Five plays

FIVE PLAYS

by

MICHELENE WANDOR

JOURNEYMAN/PLAYBOOKS
London & New York

rneyman Press Limited, 97 Ferme Park Road,
End, London, N8 9SA and 17 Old Mill Road,
k, NY 10994, USA. Playbooks, c/o Journeyman
Press Ltd, London

shed by the Journeyman Press and Playbooks, 1984

1 2 3 4 5 6 7 8 9 printing

CAUTION

All rights whatsoever in these plays are strictly reserved, and
application for performance, etc., should be made in the first
instance through the Journeyman Press Ltd, London.

ISBN 0 904526 90 9

Printed in Great Britain by
Biddles Ltd, Guildford, Surrey

OTHER STAGE PLAYS

Spilt Milk (in *Play Nine*, ed. Robin Rook, Edward Arnold)
Care and Control (in *Strike While the Iron is Hot*, ed. Michelene
Wandor, Journeyman Press)
Aurora Leigh (in *Plays by Women, Vol 1*, ed. Michelene Wandor,
Methuen)

BOOKS

The Body Politic (first anthology of British Women's Liberation
Writings; compiler; Stage One, 1972)
Understudies (on theatre and sexual politics, Methuen, 1981)
Plays by Women (editor, three vols, 1982, 1983, 1984, Methuen)
Upbeats (poems and stories, Journeyman, 1981)
On Gender and Writing (editor, Pandora Press, 1983)

CONTENTS

To Die Among Friends, *page 1*

The Old Wives' Tale, *page 45*

Whores d'Oeuvres, *page 67*

Scissors, *page 91*

Aid Thy Neighbour, *page 115*

TO DIE AMONG FRIENDS

Mal de Mere
Joey
Christmas
Pearls
Swallows

To Die Among Friends was first performed as a complete sequence in 1973, by Paradise Foundry, directed by Malcolm Griffiths, with Mike Laye, Hilton McRae, Judy Monahan, Anna Mottram, Pat Rossiter and Linda Spurrier, lighting by Del Trew. *Mal de Mere* was first performed earlier in the same year, by Portable Theatre Workshop, as part of a show called *Point 101*, to which seven writers contributed.

To Die Among Friends was first published in **Sink Songs** in 1975 (Playbooks); *Mal de Mere* is also published in **Play Nine**, edited by Robin Rook (Edward Arnold, 1981).

Mal de Mere

There are two women in this play, A and V. The action is played in a circle with invisible edges. In the original production this was marked by lighting. The only prop was one chair in the circle. A remains throughout in the circle, while V moves in and out of it as necessary. The play ends with a struggle in the circle between A and V during which A struggles to free herself from V. At the end A breaks free, leaving V in the circle, mute. It is from outside the circle that A speaks her last line.

Section 1

A: I can't get out, I can't get out, I can't get out.

V: Jenny, Jenny, can you come out to play?

A: I can't come out, she's not feeling well, I can't get out.

V: Jenny's Mum, Jenny's Mum, can Jenny come out to play?

A: She can't, it's raining, she may catch a cold, it's hot, she may sweat and get over-heated, she's just going to have her bath, she can't come out to play.

V: Jenny's Mum, please, I cordially invite Jenny to a birthday party at 4 Targill Road, where games and food will be played and eaten. From 4–6 pm, please reply to 4 Targill Road.

A: She can't come, my stomach's delicate, Jenny's stomach is delicate and grandma is coming to tea and we're having trifle and egg and cress sandwiches for tea and I can't come.

V: Good morning, Jenny's Mum, can you tell me why your daughter has attended only five days of school so far this term?

A: Jenny has troubles, Jenny is delicate, Jenny catches colds in her tummy, Jenny is a sensitive child, Jenny loves school, Jenny would go if she could.

V: She's losing valuable time at school, valuable learning time. You realise this will affect her later in life?

A: Oh, Jenny loves reading, Jenny reads all the time, anything she can lay her hands on; of course, not them comics, you never know what smut may be in them, but Jenny reads all the time, no-one could be more aware than I of the importance of a normal school life for a healthy young girl, but Jenny is far from being a normal healthy young girl, she loves school, she . . .

V: That Mrs Roberts really spoils her kid.

A: Jenny isn't spoiled, oh, no. Mummy, it's Monday, I don't feel well. Well, of course she can stay in bed for today. You'll be better tomorrow. What do they want me to do, neglect her?

V: Her Mum and Dad think she's a genius. Skinny little thing. When she's not stuffed fat with doughnuts. Plays with herself too.

A: You should see how brave she is. It isn't her fault.

V: Jenny, Jenny, flat as a penny, can't skip, can't run, can't bake a currant bun.

A: Makes you weep, makes your heart ache, makes you weep blood, makes your heart bleed tears.

V: She can't even string two sentences together at her age, little length of string, all skin and bone. Moody in school, doesn't know how to make friends.

A: She writes little stories when she's feeling well enough. It's so hard for her.

V: They think she's beautiful, a genius.

A: Poor little Jenny, what does the world want you to do? As soon as she's well, she runs and skips like any other child of her age. Of course she has problems other children of her age don't have, she's a sensitive child, she's afraid of dogs, she gets tired easily, she catches cold easily. I'm always telling her to do exercises so she'll get big and strong but she's too ill to do them regularly. 'Look, Jenny,' I say, 'look, Jenny, arms out to your sides and breathe in, arms back to your sides and breathe out,' she does them when she can, she's such a brave little thing, she never wanted to be ill. Those other children are so rough, they hurt her, all those years of hard work, why was I burdened with a sick child?

Section 2

V: Jenny's Mum, Jenny's Mum, where's my supper? Home from a hard day's slog to find you closeted up there with the fucking kid, doesn't a husband have a right to a little attention, a right to some of his rights, a right to eat after a hard day slogging his guts out? Leave the kid alone for five minutes, don't you ever leave the kid alone for five minutes? Make my supper, I'll tell her a story.

A: Tell me a story, Daddy, I'm tired of reading.

V: What did you do today, Jenny?

A: It was windy, so I stayed in bed.

V: Time was when your Mum and me climbed up Mount Ararat with ruck-sacks on our backs, the wind in our heads, our feet throbbing, our hearts pounding. She didn't mind the wind then. But times change. When I was a boy in Europe my parents bred geese for pate, when they were killed there was always a smell of singed feathers, of meat, blood . . .

A: Daddy, Daddy, can I go there?

V: No more, no more, stop bothering the child, can't you see she's tired?

A: Daddy, I want to go out to play, Mummy, can I go out to play?

V: She's too ill, that's why not. Had to cut our holiday short and come home a week early because of her.

A: Mummy, *why* can't I paddle?

V: You'll catch cold if your feet get wet. God knows I try.

A: Mummy, I'm hungry.

V: I sit up at night listening for her breathing. Ever since she was a tiny baby. I'm never out of the house for more than an hour at a time. I haven't had an evening out since she was born.

A: Do you know they read books at school? At the school I went to last week, they read books. I read books too. I didn't know school was reading books. I like the bit of school where they read books.

V: So wonderful, so healthy, she rides her bicycle to school every day, she plays games, she's developing, well, I do the housework, shop, clean, help my husband in the garden, well, you get a bit lonely when your children start to grow up, she's been so much better since she matured.

A: Atishoo.

V: Wrap up warm, you're catching a cold.

A: I'm going out.

V: You're not going out, you're catching a cold. You've got to look after yourself, you're not very strong.

A: Let me go, I'll be late.

V: No, you won't be late. You just get into bed and have a little rest. If you won't look after yourself properly, I'll do it for you. You'll thank me for it later.

A: I must get out.

V: Of course you must, I'm not stopping you. You must look after yourself. Now go to bed, and I'll bring you a nice hot fruit drink.

A: I'm going out.

V: You're not.

A: I'm going out. Get out of my way.

V: You're not going out. You can't go out. You're going to bed and I'm going to look after you and make you better.

A: Let me go.

V: No.

A screams.

V: Stop that, stop being hysterical, stop it.

A continues.

V: You stop that at once or I'll call an ambulance. They'll take you away and calm you down. You're abnormal, you stop doing that, it's not normal. You're lucky the neighbours can't hear you. Now you go upstairs and have a little rest. Mummy will look after you.

A is sobbing and exhausted.

V: Jenny's going to be in her school play, Jenny is so happy, Jenny's passed all her exams, all her teachers are so pleased with her.

A: I passed all my exams and came top in two.

V: Very talented and self-centred, finds it hard to make friends, she should learn to curb her moods for the sake of others, shows great promise, Miss Bart, headmistress.

Section 3

V: Jenny's going on a walking tour at Easter with a friend. My little Jenny. Growing up. But she'll always be my little Jenny.

A: Jane and me talk about sex with the lights off. Jane plays hockey and is very popular. Jane is my friend. She always comes to my house to talk because she's afraid her Mum will hear us. We talk about all sorts of things to do with sex. Jane goes out with boys and tells me all about it.

V: Do you like Arthur? I like Arthur. I'm going to talk to him at break tomorrow and see if I can get him to take me home from the school dance.

A: My Mum won't let me go to the school dance. She says it's too late.

V: Can't you sneak out?

A: Yes. Alright.

V: Jenny, Jenny, will you come for a ride on my motorbike?

A: Yes, alright.

V: Jenny, my Mum and Dad are out tonight, will you come back to my house and have sausages and chips?

A: Yes, alright.

V: Jenny, I like you.

A: I like you.

V: We could go into the bedroom; my Mum and Dad have got a double bed. It's much more comfortable.

A: Yes, alright.

V: Where were you? You didn't come back till four in the morning. Where were you? You had me worried sick.

A: I was out. At a party. With my friends.

V: I called the police, you know.

A: Leave me alone.

V: They couldn't find you.

A: Why don't you leave me alone?

V: How could you do this to me?

A: I'm alright, leave me alone.

Section 4

V: He's a lovely young man, such a promising future. A bit wild, but he'll settle down. The baby is beautiful. Reminds me of Jenny when she was born. Now Jenny's settled down she'll really learn what life's about. Jenny's not too well just now, what with all the work and worry, the worry and strain, a tiny baby and Jenny still so young herself. Still, as long as I've got my health and strength I can pop over there, do a bit of shopping, help her out a bit, help look after the baby. After all, what are mothers for?

A: Will you do the shopping?

V: Isn't your mother coming?

A: I don't want her to come.

V: Well, there isn't anyone else.

A: Please stay with me, sit next to me, hold my hand.

V: I can't. I've got to go to work, we've all got things to do, work to do. I'll be late.

A: Don't leave me now.

V: Don't worry, your mother will be here soon. A bit of help and company for you.

A: Please don't go. I can't get out.

V: You'll be alright for half an hour. Half an hour, she said.

A: Yes, I know. But I can't get out.

V: Of course you can't, you're not feeling well. You'll be alright.

A: The machine won't let me.

V: What machine? There isn't any machine.

A: No, there isn't. Please stay.

V: I'll be late. Hope you feel better.

A: Machines or something.

V: Your mother will be here in a minute.

A: I don't want her.

V: There isn't anyone else.

A: The mice run over everything in the night. Their feet touch everything.

V: Sssh, Mummy's here.

A: The spiders are eating their way through to my eyes.

V: Have a nice hot drink.

A: They can't get in.

V: Perhaps there's a new pill.

A: I can't get out.

V: Shall I call the doctor?

A: The rose branches are pointing their spikes in through the window.

V: Mummy won't let anyone hurt you.

A: The smell is suffocating me.

V: Mummy's baby.

A: I want to get out.

V: Sssh, lie still, you'll tire yourself.

A: Please let me out.

V: Hush, hush, hushabye baby, on the tree-top; when the wind blows . . .

A: It wants to get out of my head . . .

V: . . . the cradle will rock . . .

A: Let me out.

V: . . . when the bough breaks . . .

A: Thorns make me bleed.

V: . . . the cradle will fall . . .

A: Real blood, sharp, red, real, like real blood . . .

V: . . . down will come baby . . .

A: It's real . . . my blood is real blood . . . I must get out . . .

V: . . . cradle and all . . .

Section 5

A: My name is Jenny.

Joey

A male and a female. The male is J, the female is M.

J: Joey, Joey, can you come out to play.

M: Joey can't.

J: Joey, come and play football. I've got a new Action Man.

M: We're going to Aunt Maggie's and he'll get all muddy. Joey, put that cat down this minute, you'll get hairs all over your shirt. And just look at those shoes already.

J: Joey, you can ride my bicycle.

M: Such a rough little boy.

J: He's my best friend.

M: Roguish little eyes. Cheeky dimple.

J: We're going to play cowboys and Indians.

M: Either out with the boys or chatting up those girls from the comprehensive. Always with his elders.

J: I'm his best friend.

M: If I catch you smoking I'll beat you black and blue.

J: You'd trip over your own toenails, clumsy blowsy Mumsy.

M: Do better to learn some manners. Get a girl into trouble one day.

J: Don't care. Manners is silly and you can't come with us. We don't like girls.

M: Needs a man about the place to discipline him.

J: You can't come, you'll get your frilly dress all muddy, get mud on your knickers, pull your knickers down and see what you've got.

M: He'll settle down one day.

J: Why can't Joey come?

M: I'm not stopping him. I can go too if I want. I've got my own invitation.

J: Why don't you go, then?

M: My Mum says you're too rough.

J: Liar, liar, pants on fire, cowardy cowardy custard, fingers smell of mustard.

M: You think you know it all.

J: I do, I do, I do. You want what I know. You can't have it. We don't want you.

M: Don't want to play anyway.

J: Oh yes you do.

M: Oh no I don't.

J: Oh yes you do.

M: Oh no I don't.

J: Oh no you do.

M: Oh yes I don't.

J: As long as I play with you, you'll have to play with me.

M: Can't force me.

J: Can. If I make a move you make a move too. Tied your belt to my bike.

M: I'm not playing.

J: Are. See.

M: You're stupid.

J: Go on, run faster.

M: Bet you couldn't walk a tightrope across Niagara Falls.

J: Could. Saw your knickers when you sat on the swing.

M: You're stupid.

J: My book says you're a paranoid moralist. Catch.

  Pause.

M: Your hair's all long and curly.

J: Why won't you stand up for yourself?

M: It's all silky, just like a girl's.

J: Don't call me names, silly bitch.

M: You sound just like my Dad.

J: Coward. Salt tears, pucker lips.

M: Big bully. Your skin is all soft, like a baby's. Oh, look, goose pimples.

J: Go on, let him go.

M: No. No.

J: I want him to come to a party with me. Play cowboys and Indians. Boys together. Have a fag in the bog, chat up the birds, throw egg and cress sandwiches at each other.

M: No.

J: Don't want you with us all the time. Can't a boy have some time on his own?

M: We're playing mothers and fathers. Go away.

J: Joey doesn't like it really.

M: Joey likes me more than he likes you. You don't like Joey at all. You just want to take him away from me. You don't understand him. I understand him. I shall tell him about you. He thinks you're his friend.

J: I'm the Indian and he's the sherriff.

M: Joey plays the doctor and I play the nurse.

J: Then he's the Indian and I'm the sherriff.

M: Joey plays the Daddy and I play the Mummy.

J: There's no girls in cowboys and Indians. You can't even shoot.

M: You ought to be grateful to me.

J: Why, stupid?

M: Because I'm ever such a good audience. I listen to everything you say.

J: You're a silly cow. Stupid games. Doctors and nurses.

M: You noticed them, didn't you. Have you seen my new copy of Alice? Big pictures you can colour in. I've done two. Do you want to do one?

J: I don't care about your stupid books. Which one?

M: Come here and I'll show you. This one.

J: No. I want to do this one.

M: Alright.

J: Is this all the pencils you've got? I like crayons.

M: That's all that came with the book.

J: Oh, alright then.

M: This one's blue. Look.

J: Hey — look, you've gone and messed it all up now. And look — look at all these others — you can't paint Alice with brown arms and red hands.

M: It's not painted. It's pencils.

J: Girls. I don't want to colour your stupid book.

M: Joey did that one.

J: Which one?

M: The one with the brown arms and red hands.

J: Don't be dumb. Joey wouldn't do a dumb thing like that.

M: He did.

J: He didn't. Where is he?

M: I won't tell you.

J: Where is he?

M: He's out playing football.

J: No, he isn't. Where is he?

M: He's gone to a party.

J: No, he hasn't. I've come to get him.

M: He's here. Behind me. You'll have to reach round me to touch him.

J: Where? I can't feel him.

M: You don't want Joey, do you? You want me. You want me, don't you?

J: No, I don't. I hate you.

M: But you want me, don't you? You never liked Joey anyway. You can't cuddle Joey like you can cuddle me. That was all a game, wasn't it? Just to get me interested.

J: You don't like Joey. You don't like anyone. You just like yourself.

M: I like you.

J: You only like me if I take notice of you.

M: You don't notice me unless I'm doing what you want me to do.

J: But you don't really like me.

M: Yes, I do, I do, I like you. Why won't you let yourself admit you like me?

J: I don't like girls.

M: Yes, you do. You pretend you don't, but I know what you'd really like to do.

    She whispers.

J: You're disgusting.

M: You told me about it.

J: You're disgusting.

M: Do you want to do it to Joey, then?

J: Shut up.

M: But I thought you loved him.

J: He's my friend. Joey is my friend.

M: But you only want me, don't you?

J: You piss me off.

M: So you do have feelings for me.

J: If you call those feelings.

M: Does Joey piss you off?

J: Dumbbell, Joey's my friend.

M: You are a slippery person.

J: What do you know about me.

M: Everything. I notice every little thing, every little detail.

J: Alright, spotty miss clever, so tell me about me.

M: You know all about you.

J: No, no, go on now you've started. All this clever coy stuff, let's have it.

M: You're lazy. You dream a lot. And Joey is always the hero, and he's always right and always strong and always your friend. And then you wake up and it's cold and draughty and all the bedclothes have fallen off onto the floor, and the rain is coming in through the window. And you don't like that at all.

J: You're talking about yourself. Guys and dolls, mothers and fathers, doctors and nurses.

M: That's no dream.

J: I don't want you messing around.

M: Let me like you. Really.

J: Leave my dreams alone.

M: Of course, there is another way out.

J: What's that?

M: Marry me.

J: Where's Joey?

M: Marry me.

J: Why?

M: Marry me and you'll find Joey.

J: Where is he?

M: Marry me and you'll find out.

J: And then what?

M: Then you'll find out. How much do you like Joey?

J: Joey is my friend.

M: Any friend of yours . . . Do you love me?

J: I love you. Joey is my best friend.

M: I like Joey best of all the boys.

J: Isn't she beautiful, Joey? Be her friend too.

M: I love you, Joey.

J: I love you both.

M: Joey, will you make love to me?

J: I think it's all cool.

M: I want to be a special person to you, Joey. Make me feel like a real person.

J: My book says I am extremely liberal.

M: Joey, it's alright.

J: It's alright, Joey, I'm watching.

M: Joey, why won't you? Why not?

J: Joey, where are you?

M: I told you what I wanted. I hate you. Love me.

J: Why won't you love us?

M: I want Joey.

J: Joey, you're mean. You didn't let me be liberal.

M: Joey, you're mean, you didn't make me feel like a real person.

J: Joey —

M: Yes?

J: Please, Joey —

M: My name isn't Joey.

J: Joey?

M: My name is —

J: Nasty Joey.

M: Mean Joey.

J: He was nasty to you.

M: And you.

J: It's all your fault.

M: I hate Joey. You hate me.

J: I don't. I just want Joey.

M: You hate me.

J: We've still got each other.

M: I want Joey.

J: But I just told you. You've got me.

M: Maybe he's got someone else.

J: Someone else?

M: Someone else. Another friend. With long sensitive fingers . . .

J: I don't mind if you touch her hand.

M: Liar. You do. You want me all to yourself, don't you?

J: I don't mind. I like everybody.

M: I don't believe you. Do you love me?

J: Of course.

M: I'm tired of being married to you.

J: Where is Joey?

M: I don't care. You danced with him all evening.

J: So?

M: It's not right. You only did it to stop me dancing with him.

J: How do you know?

M: You went home with me in the end. Why didn't you go home with him?

J: I don't believe in that kind of thing.

M: I do.

J: Not for myself, I mean.

M: Liar, liar, pants on fire, nose is as long as a telephone wire.

J: I'm not.

M: Yes, you are. You want us both but you go home with me.

J: I love you both.

M: I don't stand in line for anyone. I come first.

J: I want you both ways.

M: Then let me have what I want.

J: I'm not stopping you.

M: You are. You watch Joey all the time. You watch me.

J: That's in your head, not mine.

M: Your eyes are in your head, not mine.

J: Why not be promiscuous for a change?

M: I don't want to run races.

J: Yes, you do, if I say so.

M: I'm tired of you.

J: We all have to lie.

M: Speak for yourself.

J: I do.

M: You lie for yourself. You've given yourself up. You know that?

J: I'm looking for Joey.

M: You're just greedy.

J: I don't want you.

M: See? I was right.

J: Joey is my friend. And he's coming with me. You'll see, bat.

M: He sees through you. Joey sees through you.

J: I know. That's alright. He's strong enough. He wins all the races. I want to run with the winner.

M: Don't you want to have a place of your own? Something real, no races?

J: I'm easy. I'll take Joey as long as he's there. It doesn't hurt him. He's nice.

M: I think it's all or nothing.

J: Then you know what you'll end up with, don't you?

M: Smug bastard.

J: You know I'm right. Joey!

M: You're wrong.

J: Face it. Joey!

M: Joey is better than you.

J: I hate you. I'm going to hurt you.

M: Joey will come back.

J: Of course he will. And he'll go away again.

M: Don't you mind?

J: Not much time, take what you can get. Joey!

M: You're wrong.

J: So are you.

M: I've got nothing more to say to you.

J: Till next time. Joey! Joey!

M: Don't count on me.

Christmas

Cast of two, male.

A: How many Christmas presents are you getting?

B: Oh, I don't know.

A: You don't know? You must know.

B: Some.

A: How many?

B: About seven or thirteen.

A: I'm getting at least about a hundred exactly. Don't you have Christmas in your house?

B: Yes, we have it in our house when they have all those special programmes on the tele.

A: I'm getting about two hundred presents; and they're all big. Don't you know what Christmas is?

B: 'Course I do, stupid. Christmas is next week.

A: You're stupid. Christmas is when Jesus the saviour of the world was born, he was a little tiny baby and he was born in a warm stable and all the animals were low down and the three kings came and gave him presents. That's what Christmas is about and that's why we get all our presents. Aren't you getting any at all?

B: I said, Mum said we'll get something. I'm having new pyjamas.

A: Oh, your Mum can give you those. Isn't your Dad giving you a bike or a table tennis set or a football outfit, or something big like that?

B: Look.

A: What?

B: Conker. A forty-fiver. Jimmy Grange tried to take it away from me at break but I tied it round my belt and the string was too strong.

A: Jimmy Grange is getting a speedboat for Christmas. A real one.

B: No, he isn't.

A: Yes he is. He said.

B: He tells everybody that. But his Mum told him off for it.

A: Well, he said it's true.

B: It isn't.

A: It is.

B: Isn't.

A: Is.

B: Isn't.

A: Liar.

B: Not. Ask his Mum.

A: I think conkers is childish.

B: We're making all our own decorations, silver glitter and gold stars. Uncle Mike showed us how to make real lanterns. With candles inside.

A: Our tree is so big my Dad had to ask the man who delivered it to bend it over to get it through the door.

B: Jimmy Grange plays on my side in football.

A: You're coming to have tea with me tomorrow.

B: I'll have to ask my Mum.

A: I'll tell her. She can collect you at about half-past six; not before because I want you to watch Nationwide with me. My mother can make us sausage rolls for tea.

B: I can stand on my hands.

A: Oh dear; I've got a headache.

B: Can you do this?

A: I shall go home. Mummy always draws the curtains when I have a head-ache. Everyone has to be quiet.

B: I can walk on my hands as well.

Pause.

Last week the policeman came and told us all about kerb drill. He came back this week with Jimmy Grange's Mum. She was crying. Jimmy went off with them. Jimmy had a whole box of sweets. He had to carry it in both hands.

A: And then when we've been quite good, not very good, but done our work quite well, we get half a good mark, and if we're very good and have done our work very well, we get a whole good mark. At the end of the term the boy with the most good marks is top of the class. I keep my uniform very clean. I'm going to be a prefect when I'm in the top form.

B: Jimmy got probation. I wanted to see the inside of a dungeon, but they didn't put him in a dungeon. His Mum cried again. She always waits for him at the school gates now. We threw gravel at her yesterday so Jimmy could come with us to the bomb site. His Dad came after him though. He's good at football, Jimmy's Dad.

A: Touch my finger. Now we're blood brothers. We'll always be friends. You'll always be my friend.

B: Blood does look funny.

A: Mummy, he never has any presents to show me.

B: I'm saving all my pocket money and when I'm old enough I'm going to do a paper round and when I grow up I'll buy an E-type Jag for my Dad and some diamonds for my Mum.

A: And I've got £500 in the bank already. From my grandmother's side, you know, and there will be a lot more when she dies. I'm not awfully fond of football. It's such a dirty messy game. I don't think I was born to play games. I'm much better at using my mind. Do you know how babies get inside the Mummy and then come out? I've got some pictures in one of my books.

B: I can hear my Mum and Dad's bed creaking every Saturday night. I saw my sister Janet an hour after she was born. She looked horrible. I kissed Jennifer behind the gymnasium today.

A: We're going to Ireland for Easter, and I shall learn to ride a horse.

B: Let's go to the cinema.

A: I'll ask Madelaine. She lives next door.

B: Jennifer and me usually go in the stalls.

A: Oh, no, not the stalls. One doesn't take a girl in the stalls.

B: Lend us a pound, then?

A: Chap ought to give a girl the best. They expect it.

B: Pay you back tomorrow.

A: They won't come up with the goods otherwise. You know what to do?

B: What do you mean?

A: Well . . . you know, at the slushy bit you take her hand and sort of squeeze it.

B: Oh yes?

A: Then you slip your arm round her shoulders. Then afterwards you help her on with her coat and just sort of keep your arm there. If you're lucky she'll let you kiss her outside her front door.

B: My Mum and Dad have gone up the pub. We're going to fuck in my bedroom.

A: I say, she doesn't . . .

B: Yeah. She's alright.

A: I say, could I take her out one night?

B: Yeah. Be my guest. I'll ask her for you, if you like.

A: Look — you don't want to marry her, and all that?

B: Oh, no. Jennifer's a friend.

A: I'm going to marry a girl with land.

B: I want my wife to be a virgin when I get married. Wouldn't want to think my woman had been laid by layabouts like you and me, eh?

A: Yes, quite.

B: Come on, they're always late. Pint?

   Pause.

A: Of course, the vacations are meant for working. But it is nice to look up old friends.

B: Day release, one day a week. Stuck in this place full of little snobs who couldn't do a day's real work to save their lives. Stinks like school. Poncy little nobodies.

A: Then I shall probably take a course in management consultancy. I know this escort agency, couple of dollies . . .

B: Not anywhere too — you know — I'm . . .

A: Of course, old chap; small and cosy. How much have you got on you?

B: Fifteen quid. Payday yesterday.

A: That'll be ample, old boy.

B: Has to see me through the week.

A: Come on, can't keep them waiting. Gin and orange? Double brandy?

B: Bitter. Pint.

A: Come on, girls, we'll take a box. Choccy?

B: So fucking cool. Could chill your drink on the back of her hand.

A: Pretty boring pair of dollies. Oh, well, last lap coming up. We'll go to my pad, eh? Taxi . . .

B: Sat close to her in the theatre and restaurant. Arm kept brushing mine. I could tell she was wearing make-up — well, you could smell it — but I couldn't tell where. Her eyes were deep blue, with black, black lashes and every time she moved near to hear what I was saying there was this cloud of, sort of scent, all those flowers in the wind, streams and meadows. And she listened to what I said like it was the greatest thing she'd ever heard. She kept making me want to touch her and my hands were sweating and I didn't dare sit too near her in case she could smell me sweating. But she kept moving close and listening and leaning —

A: We'll toddle off to the bedroom, old chap.

B: Wasn't there in the morning.

A: You must have passed out, old chap. Overcome, eh? Oh, they never stay, you know. Real mover, yours. Mine was a bit like a wet flannel. Lay there as though she was waiting for a bus. By the way, it's ten quid for the extra.

B: Extra?

A: Sure. It's not free, you know.

B: You mean — they — ?

A: Come off it, don't play the country mouse.

B: She did it for money?

A: Wake up, lad. They all do it for money. Whether it's fish and chips or the old Trattoria. How else does a girl get around. Why, your mother —

B: You leave my mother out of this.

A: My mother too. It's not personal. It's the way things are.

B: It's disgusting.

A: Not if you can use it, get something out of it yourself. It's all money. Her face, her clothes, the way she moves. Money. All of it. Make the most of it while it lasts. How old is she? Twenty-four, twenty-five? It'll be all over by the time she's thirty, over the top. Never know, might end up with one of them myself. They do know how to please a man. After all, it's their job. I admire professionalism.

B: I want a girl who's real. A real person.

A: Real comes out of a bottle. Money makes them real. Blonde hair only looks that real when it's really expensive. All those birds you go out with just imitate that little taste you had last night. That's the real thing. And the others know it. You enjoyed it, didn't you. She was good, wasn't she?

B: How do you know?

A: Well, I didn't listen at the door.

B: Christ.

A: Cheer up. Another twenty-five quid and you can have another dish of the same.

B: It's all very well for you, isn't it?

A: It's there for the taking.

B: Management consultant. In line for Daddy's firm. Even if I wanted it I couldn't have it.

A: Give you a job, if you like. Like to see a lad with initiative . . .

B: Yeah?

A: Yes. What can you do? Experience?

B: French polisher; skilled. Five years' experience. Some private work on the side restoring antiques. Detailed, skilled work. Beautiful craftsmanship in those old objects. Men who made them never got a chance to use them. Any more than I do.

A: Man of taste, eh? Problems of going over to machinery . . . modern furniture factories, not much scope for the old individual treatment . . . If I don't give you a job now you'll soon be made redundant by automation anyway . . . stately homes are dying out too. Not much call for inlay work nowadays . . . foreman at fifteen hundred?

B: To keep a wife and kids?

A: Well, you can still do a bit on the side . . . I believe it's an increase on what you're getting now, anyway?

B: Cost of living's gone up 25% overall this year; food's gone up 40%, only eat meat once a week, a mortgage, two kids, the wife's been sacked because she's pregnant again. Bit on the side?

A: With overtime you could make it up to £2,250. Every problem has its solution.

B: Very little choice; I could try it for a while. Nothing to lose. And things are getting worse.

A: Wonderful; knew you'd see things our way. Splendid. Good to have you with us. We'll go a long way together. After all these years. Play your cards right, get on well with the lads, good bunch of chaps, and other perks might come your way. Old friends must stick together. Tea-parties and conjurers, eh?

B: Went to the same school. Lived three streets apart, and in some ways might have been separated by an ocean for all the families mixed. Still. Things change. Let's have a drink on it, eh?

A: Er — well, maybe not just now, old chap. You see, at work and all that — it wouldn't do to be seen hobnobbing, having a drink together. Might — er — damage your credibility with the lads. Times change. You understand.

B: Didn't teach us much at school, never made it interesting. Couldn't wait to get out and earn some money. I suppose he must have been brighter. Or maybe the teachers were more his sort in the first place. Home from home.

A: Wonderful having someone I can trust on the shop floor; sniff out the insurrection before it happens, eh?

B: Got thrown out of university. Walked straight into the director's chair.

A: Come over on Sunday and bring the kiddies. Open house.

B: He's happy now. Rolls in at eleven, leaves at four. Never seen his pay slip. Worked seventeen hours overtime last week. The whole factory. Export order.

A: Cigar, old chap? Tell me, do you think young Grange is trying to stir something up? Any links with the reds on Clydeside?

B: He doesn't know what's going on. Not at all. Not a dicky.

A: Don't bring me the gen at work. Ring me at home — after eleven at night.

B: There's nothing to worry about. Nothing at all. No more trouble than I can handle over a pint with the lads. He doesn't know what's coming to him.

A: What do they do in their spare time? You know, which ones go for the dollies — a bit on the side, the wife doesn't know; is there anyone who you know — er, prefers to be with the chaps.

B: Never think we used to undress in the gym together.

A: Going to switch from weekly wages to piece-rates. Turkey dinner at Christmas and a visit to the Palladium for their families. Profits dropped this year; only made £300,000.

B: Average overtime's risen by five hours per man per week.

A: I dream about it. It's like working overtime.

B: The wife says she'll dump the kiddies on the boss if I don't get home earlier on Fridays and stop going in on the weekend. What can I do?

A: Susan is a simply wonderful little housekeeper. She'll be past her best in a few years, of course. But Father's just married again . . .

B: Wife's gone home to her mother. Well, what with the strike coming up — not that she doesn't think it's right. Says there's nothing she can do; tired of waiting for me to come in late. Threw a right one; flung one of her boots across the room and bust the mirror. Didn't know she was brewing up. I suppose she has a hard time, with the kids all day. Somehow I don't have time to worry about them.

A: You knew about it all the time.

B: On Tuesday we gave him an ultimatum; amount of rise; changes in conditions and hours; no more compulsory overtime to make the wages up to a livable minimum. Gave him the fucking works.

A: Where's your loyalty?

B: Occupied when they refused to negotiate. Took charge of the whole lot. Got people down from all over the country; support, telling us what happened in their strikes . . . problems with scabs; most of them didn't see it's the long term we've got to think of, not just the wage this week or this month.

A: You just had a raise. Whose side are you on?

B: Listed grievances: no real pay rise as such for the last two years. Not sufficient to equal the rise in the cost of living. Inadequate heating; no bogrolls. Of course those were demands we put to *him*. In the end we want control in the hands of the people. To him that's all propaganda; no point in flinging that at him. Easy does it. More important to strengthen ourselves, than worry about convincing him.

A: After all I've done for you. If it wasn't for me, you'd have no jobs.

B: If it wasn't for us he'd have no profit.

A: Tennis club, pension schemes, Christmas dinner and the Palladium.

B: He gets better and better off and we get worse and worse off.

A: Only factory in the area. Free anti-flu injections when the scare was on. I could take you to the Industrial Relations court.

B: This'll be a nice Christmas present for him.

A: We've been advised to settle.

B: Just like being kids again.

A: Meet half your pay claim. Conditions will be improved on the following time scale.

B: Five weeks of occupation; it's been hard. Some of the wives have put pressure on the lads to give in. Most of them have come up a treat. Support all the way. Bringing us food and fags and stuff.

A: Let's face it, neither you nor I can hold out much longer.

B: We squeezed a bit more.

A: I could sack you after this.

B: Been here fifteen years. Kiddies at school.

A: I can find ways of forcing you.

B: He could never understand there were people who had less than him.

A: Put shit through your letter box.

B: He's closer to the edge than you'd think . . . little tilt . . .

A: There's always the secret police.

B: It's a shame really.

A: They'll find evidence. Convict you of conspiracy if they can't.

B: I can't waste time feeling sorry for his insecurities. If I reached out my hand in sympathy he'd chop it off and then retire me on an inadequate disablement pension.

A: You couldn't run the company, make the decisions, keep accounts, understand economics.

B: Try us.

A: I don't want to work eleven hours a day on a machine or out in the rain on a building site.

B: Nor do we.

A: Who's going to do all the work? Keep the country going?

B: All of us.

A: But you'll need a major reorganisation of the structure of society.

B: You're getting warm, old son. From each according to his ability, to each according to his needs.

A: I'm glad you said 'his'. I'm not doing women's work and that's final.

B: Maggie's been on about that. She says we've got to share the housework now she's out at work.

A: You'll have to sort her out.

B: It's not easy.

A: Come on, man, you're still the boss. Let's have a drink on it, eh?

B: Slap on the back, arm round the shoulders? Brothers under the skin?

A: Remember how we used to tie the dinner lady's apron to the hall door?

B: You think about it, work it out, listen to other people, and one day there's another explanation for it all, and this time it fits.

A: Brandy? Pint?

B: After the settlement: a compromise. But this isn't the end. It's the beginning for most of us.

A: Look, I didn't mean all that about sacking you. Tell you what. I'll give you a raise. No-one has to know. A private arrangement.

B: It's not up to me any more.

A: Well, must be off to Susan now. Spinach souffle with Bombe Surprise to follow. Superb cook, did I ever tell you?

B: She's gone off.

A: Yes, well, that escort agency's always been reliable. You'll know where to find me when you change your mind.

B: Maggie and I will have to talk seriously.

A: Beautiful dollies. Not as pert as they used to be when I was a lad, though.

B: We've been through a lot together. Since she's gone I've been thinking a lot. I'm going to have to do some listening.

A: Hunt balls.

B: The minutes of the last meeting; assess the action.

A: Like royalty I felt, the first time I made it with a bird.

B: Then the chat. Talk seriously with her. Listen. Start to work things out.

A: No-one was ever as beautiful as we.

B: Then the vote; can't leave our marriage behind all the other changes.

A: Watched the autumn sun rise.

B: This'll be some Christmas present.

Pearls

A couple. HE and SHE. He sings 'Happy Birthday' and gives her a wrapped present — a box of chocolates and a pinny. These stage directions are based on Paradise Foundry's production of the plays.

HE: Make me a cup of tea.

SHE: I just made you one. *(Eating the chocolates.)*

HE: I want another.

SHE: How many cups of tea have I made you in the last twenty years?

HE: You never made me tea before we married. It was always your Mum.

SHE: I said the last twenty years.

HE: Drove me up the wall, that did. She always made it too weak.

SHE: A thousand a year; calculating three a day, that's about twenty thousand at a mean estimate. Weekends you never stop. Could be as many as forty.

HE: What about all the times I've made you a cup of tea?

SHE *(holds up both hands)*: Cut one of those off and I could still count the number of times you've made me tea.

HE: Oh, stop nagging.

SHE: I just wanted to . . .

HE: Shut up.

SHE: I haven't got anything to say to you anyway.

HE: So shut up.

SHE: I wish I'd never married you.

HE: I'd have been a lot better off. Could have had anyone.

SHE: Won an award for fastest shorthand of the year. Could have been taking dictation from executives.

HE: If I hadn't taken you on you'd still be on the shelf.

SHE: Never bothered about a career. No Alfred Marks bureau in my day. No ads on the tubes. Mostly trams where we lived.

HE: I didn't have to marry you.

SHE: Stuck in that typing pool all my life?

HE: Three kids inside three years. Must have been off my head. I ask you.

SHE: In my day you had to be responsible. No atomic bomb, no pill; young girls have it too easy nowadays.

HE: Dad was never happy.

SHE: White lace, with lilies of the valley round the veil. Mum and me made it.

HE: Mum was always miserable. Nagged at him from the minute he got home. He used to fall asleep in his armchair so he could snore louder than she talked.

SHE: Little pink babies in wicker cradles.

HE: There were a few nice days; Christmas, birthdays.

SHE: It was never how I imagined.

HE: Nothing changes. You don't find out till it's too late.

SHE: We've had a lovely family. *(Putting on the pinny.)*

HE: You bet. They couldn't wait to get out of the house.

SHE: We did our best.

HE: One in and out of trouble. Sylvie living off social security with two little bastards.

SHE: If you'd taken more notice of them when they were little . . .

HE: Bitch.

SHE: We can't complain really; flowers on our anniversary.

HE: Bitch. If it wasn't for you.

SHE: Yes?

HE: If it wasn't for you — I could have —

SHE: Could have what, dear?

HE: Oh . . . anything . . . I could have been a great . . . woodcarver.

SHE: But you made all these cupboards and bookshelves. The cocktail cabinet.

HE: I could have done big things, real things, been an artist even.

SHE: We couldn't have bought them.

HE: I could have carved the doors on cathedrals.

SHE: You don't believe in God. *(Exit.)*

HE: That's not the bloody point. I *could* have.

SHE: Well, I never stopped you. I thought you liked making things for the house. Spent enough time in the shed on weekends.

HE *(muttering)*: Only place I could be on me own with no-one telling me what to do.

SHE: What?

HE: Nothing. Nothing.

SHE enters with a bucket and mop. Starts mopping the floor.

SHE: Spent all weekend running backwards and forwards with cups of tea. Emptying ashtrays.

HE: First a house, then a car, then a colour tele . . .

SHE: You decided. You only told me afterwards.

HE: I earned the money.

SHE: Not all of it.

HE: Most of it.

SHE: You don't know how much I earned.

HE: Pin money. Who signed all the cheques?

SHE: You never paid for new curtains, shoes for the kids, my clothes, birthday cards, never gave me extra for Christmas turkeys . . .

HE: Oh, shut up.

SHE: You never asked how I did it.

HE: Blimey. You'll be telling me next you paid your way.

SHE: I did.

HE: Oh, yes? And how do you make that one out?

SHE: Housework.

HE: I mean *real* work. Money work.

SHE: I did that too.

HE: Yeah? What?

SHE: Copy. I wrote copy for cosmetics ads.

HE: Eh? You're raving.

SHE: 'Lipsticks that cling to your lips while you cling to his . . .'

HE: She's wandering.

SHE: 'The soft sweep of Charisma keeps you fresh and enticing through the day and as long as you wish all your wishes come true.' Mine. Both of them.

HE: Oh, my God.

SHE: I won the Woman's Mirror prize three years running; I had a contract with Charisma cosmetics for ten years, while the kids were growing.

HE: Oh yes. And when did you do all this poetic rubbish?

SHE: Over the stove, in the laundrette, bathing the babies, cooking your supper.

HE: Ha. Why didn't you tell me?

SHE: I've been telling you for the last five minutes.

HE: Why didn't you tell me before?

SHE: You never asked me.

HE: I don't believe you.

SHE: You can see the letters if you like.

HE: Sly old bitch. Keeping secrets from me all those years.

SHE: You'd have lit the fire with them if I'd told you. *(Dumps mop in bucket. Exit.)*

HE: I bloody wouldn't.

SHE: You've never seen anything I do.

Pause. The couple become rather younger. At the beginning of this section they are a modern 'liberated', equal couple, a bit self-stereotyped. SHE enters with a vase of flowers and aerosol spray.

HE: Darling.

SHE: Oh, darling.

HE: You are so important to me.

SHE: I'll do anything for you.

HE: You understand me so well. You are my inspiration. When you went shopping, when you were out of the house for a moment, in the garden picking chives, I couldn't write. I had to know you were there, feel the warmth of your body through the walls.

SHE: My job is to protect your work. Keeping all the hatchet-nosed journalists at bay. Being your loving jailer. The only one allowed access.

HE: The nights I had to sleep on the couch because I couldn't bear the distraction of your breathing.

SHE: Access only when you need me.

HE: I must have peace to think creatively.

SHE: His greatest successes were books for children; he revolutionised the fairy story for our time.

HE: Keep the children quiet, can't you.

SHE: It's raining. Yes, love.

HE: Read them a story or take them to your mother's.

SHE: Children queue up for your autograph. Ours saw him for an hour every evening and part of the weekend.

HE *(as if in reply to an interview question)*: Children have so much to teach us.

SHE *(arranging flowers)*: An artist needs protection from the harshness of reality.

HE *(interview tone)*: My wife has been a tremendous inspiration to me.

SHE: His work is vital.

HE: In my first book of poems . . .

SHE: I never saw them till they were in print.

HE: Most of the love poems were written to her, yes. The others?

SHE: He believes in himself.

HE: Women are beautiful. Women are perfection. I need women for my art.

SHE: It's not everyone who has the gift of inspiring beauty in others. We need artistic genius in these troubled times.

HE: A writer has much to offer in these troubled times. As an alternative to the muck of politics. An artist can give beauty where there is none. Art and politics occupy different, shall we say, lands in the map of the mind. Art is pure, eternal, universal, above the trivia of the everyday. Get the kids out of my way, stop chattering, I'm busy.

SHE: Nothing happens suddenly. *(SHE stands.)* Looking back, you can sometimes discern where changes started. I used to walk in the park when I could. Before collecting the kids from school. I used to try and write down what I felt. Sometimes they looked like poems, sometimes they were just long rambling things.

HE: Where the hell have you been?

SHE *(starts to mop again)*: Of course I knew anything I wrote wasn't as good as him. He's got real talent.

HE: The kids have been back from school a whole hour. I didn't know where the chocolate biscuits were.

SHE: And there wasn't much time, between working and shopping and cooking and all that. And him too. Children. Demanding.

HE: It's half-past bloody five.

SHE: Grass was bright green, it had just been raining. Crocuses deep purple shading into lilac shading into white. Juicy looking flowers. Windy, cold, but the sun was shining and crisp.

HE: I've lost a whole hour's work.

SHE: Well, I wrote all that down. But those words weren't important. I suppose I was beginning to look at what was outside us, at what surrounded me.

HE *(interview tone)*: Well, yes, I do believe the critic has a role in the world today.

SHE: That keeps me going for now.

HE: Yes, that was my first script. The film industry is, of course, corrupt. But my wife is a great support to me.

SHE: Then there was a gap. When a lot of things happened for which there are no images. I was no longer alone and yet I was more alone than I had ever been. It was a kind of gathering. Of forces.

HE: Where the hell have you been?

SHE: Of course, there are words for what happened. But those of us who were inside what was happening found it hard at first to speak about it. There was so much opposition. *(Mop in bucket, collects wrappings and aerosol.)*

HE: I don't like this. Bloody hen parties all the time. What do you talk about?

SHE: New choices. You wouldn't understand.

HE: A load of hysterical dykes. Why can't you leave things as they are.

SHE: What things?

HE: Things. Us. How we were.

SHE: You don't really like it any more than I do.

HE: Me? When have I complained?

SHE: Not really, you don't.

HE: Hot air. What's the matter with you. *(SHE exits.)* You've got everything a woman could want. Successful husband, lovely home, beautiful kids.

SHE *(from off stage)*: And no self.

HE: What?

SHE: I'm not the only one. *(Enters to get flowers.)*

HE: Not the only what?

SHE: Not the only one. Fed up. Had enough. Changing. Telling you what changes are necessary. You've got to change too.

HE: You don't want me to change. You want to stifle me.

SHE: Shut up and listen. For a change.

HE: Oh yes? I can't say 'chick', eye a bird's tits, have to watch what I say to you, can't criticise anything except myself. Bloody castration, that's what you want.

SHE: Doesn't seem to be doing you any harm. You've got to learn to take account of people you've taken for granted before.

HE: Like who?

SHE: Like me. *(Exit with flowers.)*

HE: Yes, well, what about all of you. While we're at it, what about all of you, eh? Cock-teasers; coquettes. Little giggles, no backbone, weak, leaning, on me, on us, we're your insurance to a cushy future, that's all we are.

SHE *(shouting)*: We don't like it any more than you do.

HE *(shouting too)*: Why don't you do something about it, then?

SHE *(shouting)*: We are; that's what you're objecting to.

SHE enters, carrying an iron.

HE: Okay. There is someone I'd rather not be.

SHE: Who? *(Starting to put a plug on the iron.)*

HE: Mr Marvel, muscleman, mortgage maker, world builder. Really, I don't . . .

SHE: What?

HE: Confession isn't my scene.

SHE: Man of action, eh?

HE: Not into laying my soul bare. That's woman's stuff.

SHE: Ah, we mustn't show any weaknesses, must we? Might lead to misunderstandings. Mustn't be less than a *real* man.

HE: Watch it. Your confidence is more fragile than you think.

Pause.

SHE: We can't do it alone.

HE: This is between us. You and me. Private.

SHE: Yes and no.

HE: The perfect answer.

SHE: Get down from your high chair.

HE: Well, what are you offering? What sort of view is there, what images can you give me so that I can see where I'm going?

SHE: There are no images. The old ones have faded.

HE: Oh no. You don't get out of it as easily as that.

SHE: Well, there is a short term and a long term. It doesn't fit into three easy sentences. And you must take part in the process too. And even if there is a picture, it doesn't explain how we get from here to there. That's the process; and while we have a picture ahead of us, we must also allow ourselves to change, as the process moves. As we move it.

HE: Jargon. Political jargon.

SHE: Anything becomes jargon if you don't want to understand it.

HE: Change is simply a matter of will.

SHE: Then why don't I get paid as much as you? Why do I do all the housework, why . . .

HE: Oh, don't bring all those silly things up again.

SHE: Acts of will, acts of God. Something has to be done, to change.

HE: Well, of course it does, woman, I know that.

SHE: Don't be so arrogant.

HE: Silly bitch.

SHE: You never thought there was anything wrong, did you? It was all very cosy for you. All the dirty work gets done by magic. You don't like seeing stinking sink-tidies, the insides of sewers, do you? You can take charge everywhere but in your own home.

HE: My home is my home.

SHE: And mine.

Pause.

HE: I don't trust you.

SHE: I don't trust you either.

HE: All that role breaking down.

SHE: I don't need you any more.

HE: All those political arguments. On and on.

SHE: I choose to work with you.

HE: Work? In bed?

SHE: Yes. Narrow the divisions.

HE: Oh yes.

SHE: Trying to be independent and responsible at the same time.

HE: What about me?

SHE: I can't see your insecurity as long as you clutch so hard at the brittle picture you have of yourself.

HE: Crack. Is that what you call politics?

SHE: Well — it's trying to bring things out of their separate boxes; to see why they are shut off from each other, and to try and make connections between them. And then change them.

HE: That's very abstract.

SHE: I told you I couldn't say it in three sentences. We can't do everything now, all at once.

HE: But you have it all your way. Speed up, slow down, yes, ma'am, no ma'am, anything you say is right, ma'am. The oppressor oppressed.

SHE: Well, you'll just have to shut up for a while. Or go more slowly; be quieter. Forget about human nature.

HE: I won't let you castrate me.

SHE bursts out laughing.

HE: It's easier for women to talk about things like that. Feelings, emotions.

SHE: You're doing ok.

HE: That's because I'm talking to you.

SHE: Well, talk to some men for a change.

HE: What kind of politics is that? Here's me, behind your politics.

SHE: I haven't forgotten you. How could I. But you must see me too.

HE: So who's winning?

SHE: It's not that kind of fight.

HE: Sorry. Just panicking.

SHE: It's always panicky when things are changing. I'm not used to it.

HE: What about the real things?

SHE: What real things?

HE: Well, we talk in our small way about liberation, political change in how we live together, attacking the myth of motherhood, changing sex roles —

SHE: Who does?

HE: We do — well, you did first, that's true . . . and look at us — a drop in the ocean; the energy it takes to make even tiny changes — like sharing the cooking.

SHE: Don't you feel any progress?

HE: Of course I do. But it's so *slow*.

SHE: One swallow doesn't make a summer. Compared to ten years ago, we've beaten the speed of light. Compared to the future we've only just started clearing out the cupboards. And there are all the other people. Other swallows.

HE: Oh come on.

SHE: I can't stand it either. I want to scream and scream and then stop and find everything suddenly different and easy. But I have to look from the past to the present, to the future and then back again. I can't stop moving.

HE: There's no choice, is there?

SHE: No. Not any more. We must go on.

SHE exits with iron. HE continues mopping the floor, starting from where SHE left off.

Swallows

Two women, one older, one younger. The older is O, the younger Y.

O: What have you got on your mind, little girl?

Y: Peeling potatoes and putting silver wires through them, putting them . . .

O: . . . on your mind, little girl?

Y: The wires of the past, the past wires . . .

O: But what exactly is it, little girl?

Y: When you leave me alone I can think. I can't think when you ask me questions all the time.

O: But I am only here to help, little girl.

Y: You're distracting me.

O: I am here to help.

Y: Your hair shines.

O: It is the light behind me.

Y: Your hair has all the colours of the rainbow in it. I cut my hair when it gets in my eyes.

O: Your eyes, little girl?

Y: The little strands of hair. They get in my eyes, I can't see with things in my eyes.

O: Can you see clearly, little girl?

Y: When I wear glasses. I wear glasses.

O: Take them off.

Y: No.

O: Take them off.

Y: No. No.

O: Take them off.

Pause. Y takes them off.

Now look at me.

Y: Your hair has glints in it.

O: You see.

Y: Your hair is a halo of glints. I can't see your hair.

O: Of course you can.

Y: I can't. I can't see you. Give me back my glasses.

O: No.

Y: Give me back my glasses.

O: No. No.

Y: Please.

O: Here you are, little girl.

Y puts her glasses back on.

Tell me about the potatoes, little girl.

Y: Potatoes? What potatoes?

O: The potatoes you told me about. The ones with silver wires through them.

Y: Oh, you are so stupid. They were then. They're not real. They were an image.

O: Why did you use an image?

Y: Because you are a fool. Because you talk like someone else.

O: Like who, little girl?

Y: Like whom, like whom.

O: Like whom, little girl?

Y: Don't call me little girl.

O: You mind my calling you little girl?

Y: It doesn't matter what I mind. Don't do it.

Silence.

Please don't.

O: Very well. Now, go on, please.

Y: On the white plates, waiting for the children to come home from school, cutting them up into chips, rinsing them under the water so they don't go brown in the air, not soaking them in water because they lose something vital.

O: What?

Y: I don't know.

O: Did you read about it?

Y: Of course I read about it. I have read about everything. I have found it for myself. No-one has taught me anything I was not prepared to know.

O: Who were the children?

Y: Children. It doesn't matter. Children. They expected things.

O: What things?

Y: The same things I expected.

O: Did you expect things?

Y: Yes.

O: When?

Y: When I . . .

O: When you were . . .

Y: When I was a little girl.

O: You may say that?

Y: What?

O: Little girl.

Y: Of course I may. It's the truth.

O: I see. Give me your glasses again.

Y: No.

O: Give me your glasses.

Y: Why?

O: I want to look at you through them.

    Y gives O the glasses.

    You did.

Y: Did what?

O: You did. I can see you.

Y: What did I do?

O: You left them.

Y: I didn't.

O: You did.

Y: I didn't.

O: Oh, but you did.

Y: I'm very careful.

O: Not this time.

Y: I'm always very careful. Always.

O: How can you be sure?

Y: I know.

O: Well, this proves it, doesn't it?

Y: No. No. One event doesn't provide a theory.

O: But you left them.

Y: I didn't.

O: You did. You left them.

Y: How do you know?

O: I saw them. They went brown.

Y: Brown?

O: They went brown. You should have put them in water after all.

Y: Water? Put what in water? What are you talking about?

O: The potatoes. You should have put the potatoes in water. They have gone brown.

Y: I wasn't talking about potatoes.

O: I was.

Y: I don't know when you are talking about.

O: The potatoes. In the plate. Waiting.

Y: They waited on the board.

O: Ah, so you lied.

Y: I'm always waiting.

O: It was a mistake?

Y: I didn't do it.

O: It was a mistake.

Y: I can't do anything on purpose.

O: You should not have put them through.

Y: What?

O: The silver threads. The wires. They tarnish the potatoes.

Y: Not the air?

O: Oh, the air too. But the brown is strongest where the wires are. The tarnish goes deepest there.

Y: It isn't tarnish, though. You can't call it tarnish.

O: I can.

Y: But it's wrong. It's not the chemical formula for what happens.

O: Well, just think of it as a figure of speech. A figure of speech.

Y: Why do you keep repeating things?

O: I do not repeat things.

Y: You do. You repeat things I say.

O: Only to bring them to your attention. You would forget otherwise. There were the potatoes, the wires, the children, the plate, the waiting.

Y: But you weren't there. You don't know.

O: Oh, but I was. I was there all the time.

Y: I didn't see you.

O: Of course you did not. But you see me now.

Y: No.

O: Oh, yes you do. You can't help it.

Y: Something has happened.

O: Yes. I am here to help you.

Y: I don't want help.

O: Of course you do. You cannot see without your glasses. You cannot hear without me. You cannot speak.

Y: You'll be calling me a little girl next.

O: I will show you how to speak.

Y: I don't want to learn.

O: Of course you do. You have just said so. Look.

Y: No.

O: Why?

Y: I don't want to.

O: You can't.

Y: I can.

O: You can't.

Y: I can. I don't want to.

O: Prove it.

Y: Why?

O: Because this is where.

Y: Is that enough?

O: Of course. You can always leave. You are free.

Y: You ask questions no-one else has asked.

O: I told you I was here to help you.

Y: You are so vague.

O: I have been the precise one so far.

Y: Only after I give you the material.

O: Exactly. I show you your own precision.

Y: What do you get out of it?

O: Nothing.

Y: Nonsense. You are rich.

O: Well, yes, in a sense. But this is basically for you. I shall learn whatever I can from it, but that is true of however I spend my time. There is nothing special in it for me. It is for you that it is special. For me you are one of many.

Y: But you keep telling me I am special.

O: For yourself you are, but not for me. We happen to converge, and there is the possibility that we shall be able to create a vision, together. But you must first speak.

Y: You insult me all the time. I speak.

O: I cannot hear you. I sense you moving. But I cannot hear you.

Y: You're deaf.

O: No; I am very sensitive.

Y: You're arrogant. And inconsistent.

O: Why?

Y: You've stopped calling me little girl.

O: You asked me to.

Y: Yes.

O: There you are.

Y: You heard me ask you?

O: Yes.

Y: You see. I speak and you hear me.

O: My dear girl, you are slow. Don't look at me, look at yourself.

Y: I can't.

O: You can. Close your eyes. Move your hands. Listen. There.

Y: Where?

O: There. The air is outside you.

Y: Let me touch you.

O: No.

Y: Let me touch you.

O: No.

Y: I can't see.

O: I shall throw away your glasses.

Y: No.

O: Yes.

Y: No.

O: Yes. I am doing it now.
     Pause

Y: You bitch. Bitch.

O: No.

Y: Bloody bitch.

O: I did it for you.

Y: Bitch. You're playing with me.

O: I want you to see.

Y: You want me to crawl.

O: No.

Y: You want me to thank you.

O: Not now. When you can see.

Y: Vampire.

O: You may thank me if you wish. When you can see. You will benefit, not I.

Y: I can still touch you.

O: You cannot see me.

Y: I will find you.

O: That is up to you.

Y: There, I've got you.

O: Have you?

Y: Ugh. It's wet. Slippery. Like rotten potato peelings. I can't grip you. Ugh.

O: Nonsense.

Y: You have no grip. I can't keep hold of you. You come apart. You're disgusting.

O: No.

Y: Is there any hot oil?

O: Why?

Y: To fry you in, give you body, give you an outside. Your skin is leaking.

O: Nonsense.

Y: But of course you can't feel it. You can only see what is outside you. You can't see what goes on inside you. You are slowly oozing away. You will have to stop looking at me so hard. I know you are looking at me.

O: I feel nothing.

Y: This is what I said. You broke my glasses and now you're being punished. You feel nothing. You can't feel anything.

O: You little bitch.

Y: You knew this would happen. Surely you must have a contingency plan. You must stay still and give me your attention, let me say what I like. What is wrong with you?

O: Nothing is wrong with me.

Y: Oh yes there is. I am the matter with you. You don't like me. You don't like what I say.

O: I am indifferent to what you say.

Y: That's what you say. But I know different.

O: You are playing with words.

Y: What else is there to do. You've taken away my glasses.

O: You can have them back.

Y: You've broken them.

O: I have not.

Y: You have. I heard you.

O: Did you see me break them?

Y: Of course not. How could I see? You took my glasses away from me.

O: I did not break them.

Y: You broke something.

O: Sound effects.

Y: How do I know?

O: You know.

Y: I knew it.

O: How?

Y: It didn't seem possible.

O: Why?

Y: Well, it isn't necessary, is it?

O: No. It is not.

Y: You thought I believed you, though, didn't you?

O: You did?

Y: A bit. I frightened you, though, didn't I?

O: Well . . . a bit.

Y: Really?

O: Yes.

Y: Really and truly?

O: Yes.

Y: I wasn't sure.

O: Well. It is past.

Y: Yes. For the moment.

O: Well?

Y: I ought to go.

O: Yes.

Y: It seems fairly pointless.

O: What?

Y: To go. Repeating the same moves. Throwing dice.

O: What is? Waiting for children?

Y: I'm not talking about children. I don't like children.

O: Why are you waiting?

Y: I'm not. My mother did. I'm not waiting.

O: You said you were.

Y: Yes, then. But not now. Now I'm not waiting.

O: Then perhaps you should go.

Y: This is getting nowhere.

O: I have nothing to say.

Y: Exactly. You have nothing to say. What is the point?

O: I am here to help you speak.

Y: I can't speak into nothing.

O: You must be able to.

Y: They would lock me up.

O: You are locked up.

Y: You twist what I say.

O: I show it to you.

Y: Bloody mirror.

O: Solid material.

Y: Not with a black cloth over it. Two objects making a negative. You are negative.

O: Of you?

Y: Of nothing.

O: Two negatives make a positive.

Y: Oh, forget it.

O: No. We are both right.

Y: You resent me.

O: Yes.

Y: I resent you.

O: Yes.

Y: But there is a difference.

O: Yes?

Y: You think you're superior because you recognise it.

O: Yes.

Y: Aren't you ashamed?

O: Well, yes.

Y: But you still do it?

O: Yes.

Y: Why?

O: There are few alternatives.

Y: Am I one of them?

O: In a sense. I have some idea of my effectiveness through your response to me.

Y: But you give me nothing to respond to. I know your name and nothing more. Nothing about you. Your life, what you have for breakfast.

O: Those things are unimportant.

Y: You're lying again.

O: You know that isn't true.

Y: I'm lying too now?

O: We both are.

Y: What else?

O: My skills are best in close contact.

Y: You are still an individual.

O: Yes.

Y: Does that disturb you?

O: Yes and no.

Y: That's the perfect answer.

O: Well . . .

Y: But why?

O: Because within my limits I have discovered how I work best.

Y: Who says?

O: I go on working after you have left. I work all the time.

Y: You make me obey you.

O: Well . . .

Y: Say please, give you my glasses, tell you things I have told no-one. And all the experience is at second hand. I know you can justify it. But it is second hand. You pick at the rag and bone.

O: You needed me.

Y: Nonsense. You need me.

O: In a sense. But I am irrelevant to you.

Y: You need me more than I need you.

O: In a sense.

Y: What sense?

O: You're still not sure that you exist apart from other people. Apart from me. You need me to learn that. I have accepted it a long time ago. I know. I therefore need you to learn other things.

Y: Me and everyone else?

O: Oh yes; I told you you were not special.

Y: I see. You leave me in the air.

O: Why?

Y: You tantalise me.

O: Then go. You are free to go.

Y: I want to be somewhere else.

O: Where?

Y: I don't know. Where everyone else is.

O: Where is that?

Y: Where the others are. I can see their hair, their eyes. They are cold. They are wearing coats. There is a feeling of excitement, tension. Something is happening. Everyone is there. I have never felt like this before.

O: How?

Y: I have a right to be here. Each of us has a right to be here.

O: Where?

Y: Everywhere; in the hall, in the rooms, in the place where we eat, in the places where we will sleep.

O: Where is it?

Y: The place doesn't matter. The wooden seats have red cushions. People are drinking soup and coffee out of plastic cups. They are waiting for tomorrow. Pieces of paper.

O: What do they say?

Y: There isn't time to read them now. We are walking through the corridors, passing and repassing each other. We smile at each other, friends and strangers alike. We all belong here, even those of us who have come from far away. Do you know what I mean?

O: One swallow does not make a summer.

Y: What gives you the right to be so cynical? You can't see it. You are afraid to see it. You sit here, and all the others like you sit in their own separate rooms. You are afraid to come together; for if you do, you'll see yourselves and each other for the first time. Why don't you come with me?

O: I shall stay. You will leave, but I shall stay.

Y: You needn't. You can come too.

O: No.

Y: Why? You are afraid, aren't you?

O: No. I am not afraid.

Y: What is it? Is it the evening? Kisses and arms? Don't you want to touch? Don't you want the right?

O: My role is defined by now.

Y: You can step outside it. You can come with me.

O: No.

Y: Why?

Silence.

I'm sorry. Of course you are right. If you come, you must come alone, as yourself, no fancy dress, no chaperone.

O: No.

Y: There is no rush. You can make up your own mind.

O: You are still here.

Y: Yes. I am waiting for you.

O: You know better than that.

Y: I don't.

O: Yes. You do.

Y: Yes. I do.

O: What is it?

Y: The children.

O: Yes.

Y: The children hold me back. I can't explain. I can't take them with me. I can't leave them behind.

O: Are you afraid of risking something?

Y: This is for me. Not for them as me.

O: And?

Y: Perhaps I'm not ready — I carry them with me everywhere, faces, hands, eyes, warning, admonishing, checking, controlling. Whenever I come to something new something old hisses at me. I can't prove anything.

O: What about everyone else? The shining people?

Y: Your words, not mine. It's the same for them too. Maybe they just cope better.

O: So you admit to the risks?

Y: What else have I been doing all this time? You have a gift for the obvious.

O: Thank you.

Y: Why don't you come too?

O: I told you. I stay.

Y: But why? Why?

O: I have no choices any more. I am too old. It is too late.

Y: You can't know till you try.

O: I know. You see, for me there would be no tension, no promise. I see what you mean, and your urgency, and I shall be with you. But it is too late for me as me. I have always worked alone, and all the mistakes I have made are my own responsibility. I could not get used to working differently now.

Y: But what if it all changed? If you no longer needed to be alone?

O: Well, that is different. Perhaps I am simply saying that I am a coward. I never used to be. But I am much older than all of you, and my first energies are no longer as they used to be. Until it is clear to me what my role is, I shall continue doing the best I can here.

Y: You're not the same as you were.

O: No. Here.

O gives Y back the glasses.

Y: Why?

O: They are unimportant. You were right.

Y: So were you.

O: The statement was yours.

Y: I don't understand the distinction.

O: Finish telling me about the children.

Y: It is whether they will survive while I am away. Spill boiling water on their feet, burn themselves with matches, run across the road into blind cars, if they will suffer because I am not there, when I will get back to them . . .

O: You have no children.

Y: But I know it is true. That is the risk.

O: I understand. I think it will become clearer, less of a risk.

Y: I can't stay here now.

O: No.

Y: I mean, the consequences will be the same for all of us. It is whether we create the consequences ourselves, or allow others to do it for us.

O: The children must learn too.

Y: Those of the mind as well as the body.

O: You cannot be free of yourself.

Y: You can't.

O: Nor can I.

Y: Nor can I.

O: Thank you. What is your aim?

Y: To die among friends.

THE OLD WIVES' TALE

The Old Wives' Tale was first performed on March 21, 1977, at the Soho Poly Theatre Club in London, with the following cast:

GERTIE	Maureen Pryor
ELLIE	Judith Fellows
KATIE	Valerie Lush
MEG	Sally Watts

Directed by Caroline Eves
Designed by Dee Greenwood
Production Manager, Inigo Riedl
Stage-managed by Amanda Ellis

The stage has three tables and chairs on it, each appropriate to its place: the canteen, GERTIE's *house and* ELLIE's *place.*

Scene One

The canteen of an Evening Institute somewhere in North London. Music: 'Little Old Lady Passing By'.

GERTIE *(enters and comes to the canteen table)*: Oh dear, what can the matter be, one old maid locked in the lavatory, she was there from Wednesday till Saturday —

ELLIE *(enters)*: I wasn't locked in.

GERTIE: You were, she was. *(KATIE enters, carrying three plain pointed witchy hats.)* You missed it, Kate, she locked herself in the loo —

ELLIE: I did not. The bolt stuck.

GERTIE: You wanted that caretaker to come and free you. Knight in a dirty corporation mac.

ELLIE: Have you got them, love?

KATIE *holds up the hats.*

GERTIE: Dettol mop rampant.

ELLIE: They're a bit plain.

KATIE: Oh, I've got stars, moons, all sorts — *(She takes out brown paper bags and spills a few glitter things onto the table.)*

GERTIE: Meg. Doesn't an old customer get any service?

Enter MEG.

MEG: 'Evening, ladies. Well, well.

GERTIE: You coming, then?

MEG: You're not really going to do it. In public?

ELLIE: Of course we are.

GERTIE: We're parched, love. Tea. Strong. Very.

ELLIE: Not too strong for me.

MEG: What are these for?

KATIE: I'm going to sew them on.

GERTIE: A star is born. *(Everyone groans.)* So? Irene Handl was no chicken when she started.

KATIE *is sorting the glitter into piles.* MEG *comes to wipe the table, and picks up the dirty ashtray to take it away. Under the ashtray is a condom.* GERTIE *sees it and picks it up.*

ELLIE: Oh, my goodness.

GERTIE: What sort of heavenly body is this?

KATIE: It was under the ashtray.

GERTIE: Someone's left you a tip, Meg. *(MEG laughs.)*

ELLIE: Disgusting.

GERTIE: Better not sew that on by mistake.

KATIE: Don't be daft, Gert.

GERTIE: How many tickets then, Meg?

MEG: Well . . .

GERTIE: Come on. Bring your boy-friend.

MEG: We've had a row.

GERTIE: That's settled, then. Two tickets. Mind you, we are the only good bit, aren't we, girls?

MEG *goes.*

I told Trevor, I told him, I said 'I won't say "Liver of blaspheming Jew".' You know what he said?

KATIE *(still looking at the condom)*: Well, it's no good to me, is it?

GERTIE: How did you know?

ELLIE: Throw it away, it's not nice.

GERTIE: Gert love, it's poetry. Poetry is always right. If I cut out 'Gall of goat and slips of yew' — he may not notice.

ELLIE: He will. He's been to university.

MEG *arrives with tea on a tray, plus three Milky Ways.* ELLIE *looks quizzical.*

MEG: It's alright. They're on me.

KATIE: They're easy on the teeth, them.

GERTIE *(hands* MEG *the condom)*: I'm afraid they haven't got a sell-by date.

MEG: No thanks, I'm trying to give them up.

She goes.

ELLIE: You've embarrassed her.

GERTIE: She's on the pill.

ELLIE: How do you know?

GERTIE: Tell by her thighs.

KATIE: Jackie's on the pill. You do put on weight.

GERTIE: If they'd had a pill in my day, I'd have been on it like a fish on a bicycle. You ever used one of those, Ellie?

ELLIE: Do you mind, I'm having my tea. How is Jackie?

KATIE: Oh, lovely, fine.

ELLIE: And Jean?

KATIE She sent these photos. *(Rummages in her bag.)* All of them walking along the beach, Jimmy in that fisherman's knit I did him. Never mind, I'll bring them next week.

ELLIE: Why don't you go and live with one of them?

KATIE: You can't mix generations these days.

ELLIE: It's their duty.

KATIE: Oh, they've asked me. But I don't think they mean it.

GERTIE: If you went to live by the sea — we could come down and paddle in our wellies.

KATIE: What, go and live in one of them old age bungalows? No thanks. You can smell them dying.

GERTIE: Eh, Ell, you've never told; what did you and Fred use? Eh? It's all water under the bridge now, you know.

ELLIE: If you must know, I never liked it much.

GERTIE: I never asked if you liked it, I asked what you did about it. It's not like the films. You must have done something.

ELLIE: I only talk to other married ladies about such matters.

KATIE: What about you, Gert?

GERTIE: Same as you. I always reckoned if I was sure, I knew where I was. Funny thing was that no-one told me you could get pregnant.

ELLIE: Oh really, Gert.

GERTIE: It's true. Mum told me when she guessed. Two years, Ernie and me, in the park by the synagogue. Home before Dad fell out the pub and no-one the wiser. Two years before I used anything.

KATIE: What a risk.

ELLIE: Immoral is as immoral does.

GERTIE: Half a century was it, your engagement?

ELLIE: We were saving up.

GERTIE: I never believed in saving. Anything.

KATIE: I'm stopping next week.

GERTIE: You should have got a proper contract off him when you married. Mean old skinflint. A bit of women's lib — that's what you need.

ELLIE: Fred and me have got a happy marriage.

KATIE: Friday. Dinnertime, Friday.

GERTIE: It has come round quick, hasn't it? You'll be free, Katie, you won't have to work for the first time for years. We'll have to celebrate.

KATIE: What am I going to do?

ELLIE: Are you going to stay with Jackie more now?

KATIE: I expect I will.

GERTIE: You won't miss the class?

KATIE: Oh no, I'll go down between, a few days here, there. It'll be alright.

GERTIE: We've only got three weeks.

ELLIE: Here, what about the cloaks?

KATIE: Trevor's getting them.

GERTIE: God knows what'll be in the pockets.

ELLIE: You've never grown up, have you?

GERTIE: Never. Still jealous cos Fred walked me home from your 21st?

ELLIE: And what's that supposed to mean?

GERTIE: Nothing. Nothing.

ELLIE: You want to burn your soapbox, you do. You got the vote, there's nothing left to preach about.

GERTIE: It's not having it. It's knowing how to use it.

ELLIE: Just furl your Commie banner up, Gert, because I know what you was flirting with before the war and it wasn't politics. All free love and bicycle rambles, you were.

GERTIE: I've always been my own woman and don't you forget that.

ELLIE: I can see why you're bitter —

KATIE: Come along, children. Jelly? Ice cream? Punch and Judy?

MEG *enters.*

MEG: More tea? It's nearly half-past.

KATIE: What was your row about?

MEG: He can't take yes for an answer.

GERTIE: Give him these.

MEG: You keep them. For old times' sake.

GERTIE: Cheeky.

At some convenient point earlier in the scene GERTIE *has taken an airmail letter out of her bag or her pocket and put it on the table.* ELLIE *now notices it.*

ELLIE: What's this? From France?

KATIE: It's a French letter. *(At this all four, even* ELLIE *hoot with laughter, covering over* GERTIE *who just stuffs it back in the pocket.)*

MEG: You certainly liven Wednesdays up. You knock the stuffing out of soft furnishings.

KATIE: How many tickets, then?

GERTIE: It's all modern, jeans — well, not us — the others . . .

MEG: Alright. If you tell me the story first.

ELLIE: We'll have cloaks as well.

Scene Two

Sometime during the following week. GERTIE *lays the table with a fringed shawl of some kind, sets out little China tea cups, arranges a candle or two on the table. A scratchy old record — Al Bowly singing 'In a little gipsy tea room'. While all this is happening, she recites the following, repeating it ad lib with different emphases.*

GERTIE: Glamis thou art, and Cawdor, and shalt be
         What thou art promised . . .

ELLIE *comes in.* GERTIE *has her back to her.*

>No, Ell, I haven't dusted.

ELLIE: I've brought a Tetley's tea bag if you're serving that China muck.

GERTIE: Katie with you?

ELLIE: I called for her. She must have left early.

GERTIE: She alright, do you think?

ELLIE: She's fine.

GERTIE: She seems a bit miserable.

ELLIE: Only natural. She's got lovely grandchildren, her own home. She's worked hard for it.

KATIE *arrives with a large carrier bag.*

KATIE: Hello, girls. I been in that new Sainsbury's — and you'd never guess what I found. *(She pulls out a photograph album.)*

GERTIE: You didn't find that in Sainsbury's?

KATIE: No, daft. I was doing out the spare room cupboard. I thought it was lost in the bombing. And I brought Jean's photos as well.

While KATIE *and* ELLIE *open the album* GERTIE *ostentatiously brings a very large mug for* ELLIE'*s tea bag.*

KATIE: Look, Ell — look, remember?

ELLIE: It was bombed next day. Oh, Katie.

KATIE: Have it, Ell.

ELLIE: I couldn't.

KATIE: Go on, it's your house.

ELLIE: There's all of us outside, Gert. I didn't hear about the house till we got to that farm — Beddows Farm. What a beginning, eh?

KATIE: There's one of you two in proper landgirls' overalls.

GERTIE: Those were the days. Let's have a look. Ell, you do look young. Fred — it's Fred. He's crying.

ELLIE: My Fred never cried.

GERTIE: His bride of three weeks going off to serve her country. He's got a handkerchief.

ELLIE: He's waving.

KATIE: That was my train page. I put all the photos with trains in them on that page. Everyone was always going off somewhere on trains. Look, there's the twins, when their school was evacuated. Like little parcels. All the mothers cried.

GERTIE: We had a good war, didn't we. Ell?

ELLIE: You spent most of it in the haystacks.

GERTIE: And you spent all of it washing the smell of cowshit off you.

KATIE: London was awful. It wasn't all like those Pathe newsreels. I remember that time I had to separate Ginny Harris and her sister-in-law in the bread queue. Screaming and scratching they were, oh, it was funny.

GERTIE: Hard work, beer and bread on those long wooden tables . . .

ELLIE: True Romance that is. That terrible National Loaf.

GERTIE: And it should never have happened. If the League of Nations had done its job — Mussolini and Hitler would have been painters and decorators the rest of their natural.

ELLIE: Here we go again.

KATIE: Harry and me — funny enough, the war was the best time we had. I missed the kids — but we had a real sort of companionship those years. It's the only time I was glad he had a weak chest.

GERTIE: I know what you mean, Katie. If Fred hadn't been sent to France in the war he'd never have gone further than Southend his whole life.

ELLIE: I didn't.

GERTIE: Didn't what?

ELLIE: Washing. I didn't wash all the time. I was writing letters.

KATIE: I kept all your letters.

ELLIE: To Fred. We kept all our letters.

GERTIE: Read them to us some time, Ellie.

ELLIE: Certainly not. They're personal.

GERTIE: You and your bleeding personal. And then you come right back from the war and can't wait to chain yourself to the kitchen sink.

ELLIE: You didn't exactly become Prime Minister.

GERTIE: Shorthand and typing's a skill you can take anywhere. Come on, girls, we may not be the grand old ladies of trade unionism, but we got work to do. *(She crooks her hands into claws, in parody of an arthritic witch. KATIE has meanwhile got the three witches' hats out, which now have two or three moons/stars on each. ELLIE has tidied the chairs so they won't get in the way.)*

ELLIE (FIRST WITCH): Thrice the brinded cat hath mewed.

KATIE (SECOND WITCH): Thrice, and once the hedge-pig whined.

GERTIE (THIRD WITCH): Harpier cries, 'tis time, 'tis time.

FIRST WITCH: Round about the cauldron go:
In the poisoned entrails throw.
Toad, that under cold stone
Days and nights, has thirty-one;
Swelter's venom sleeping got,
Boil thou first i' th' charmed pot.

KATIE: Shouldn't it be 'charmèd'?

GERTIE: Carry on.

ALL: Double, double, toil and trouble;
Fire burn and cauldron bubble.

SECOND WITCH: Fillet of a fenny snake,
In the cauldron boil and bake:
Eye of newt and toe of frog,
Wool of bat and tongue of dog:

> Adder's fork, and blind-worm's sting,
> Lizard's leg, and howlet's wing:
> For a charm of powerful trouble,
> Like a hell-broth, boil and bubble.

ALL: Double, double, toil and trouble,
Fire burn and cauldron bubble.

THIRD WITCH: Scale of dragon, tooth of wolf.
Witch's mummy, maw and gulf
Of the ravin'd salt-sea shark:
Root of hemlock, digg'd i' th' dark:
Liver of blaspheming J—

I'm skipping that bit.

KATIE *suddenly collapses onto a chair, weeping.*

GERTIE: We're so good, we've brought tears to her eyes.

KATIE: It's that list, it reminds me of the shop.

ELLIE *goes to comfort her, gives her a hanky.*

GERTIE: Couldn't you ask them if —

KATIE: They don't want me. They're very nice to me but I can tell they don't want me.

ELLIE: She'll be sixty. She's got to retire.

KATIE: I keep thinking, all those years, all that work, even after Dad left the shop to Sidney because he was a boy — and now this horrible young man's bought it. Do you know what he's done. He's chucked out all my boxes — all those labels I made — hooks and eyes and petersham, buttons and ribbons, buckles and slides — he's going to make it into a newsagents', with them horrible naked books in the window. They look at me as though I'm old.

ELLIE: We're not getting any younger, any of us.

GERTIE: Thank you, merry chops.

ELLIE: You've got to face it. We haven't got much longer.

GERTIE: We might all live till a hundred and twenty. Pigs might fly.

KATIE: I can't even ask them.

GERTIE: For a start, there's a brochure full of evening classes. You could learn — the guitar.

ELLIE: She hasn't got one.

GERTIE: Don't create obstacles. When my arthritis gets too bad, I shall have some of them shiny metal joints put in and then you and your guitar and me with my bones will busk down Hyde Park corner. Ellie can cough if she keeps in rhythm.

ELLIE: That house of yours is a bit big now, isn't it?

KATIE: But it's my home.

GERTIE: Well, when you move or pop off I'll have your bedside table. I've always fancied that.

ELLIE: Can't you see she's miserable? Let her be miserable.

GERTIE: I've decided it's Christmas. Clear the cauldron. The war is over.

There is a bottle of port, some lemons. GERTIE and ELLIE pour it, cut the lemons while KATIE sniffs herself dry. They hold their glasses up.

GERTIE: Hail.

ELLIE: Hail.

KATIE: Hail.

ELLIE: To a happy retirement, Katie.

GERTIE: To the Labour Government of 1945 and the National Health of 1947 that has blessed us with wards to get geriatric in. To gravetime and may it keep well clear of us.

KATIE: Harry had his insurance and the death grant.

ELLIE: I never thought the National Health was a good idea.

GERTIE: You think people get theirselves ill on purpose so as to get something for nothing.

ELLIE: Hospitals, surgeries — they're full, aren't they?

GERTIE: Mrs Katharine Bailey, may I have the pleasure?

GERTIE and KATIE dance, GERTIE leading. They stop now and again to sip their drinks during this next bit, while ELLIE with the coy but practised hand of an old hand drinks steadily, at some point forgetting to let go of the bottle, and then dancing with it.

ELLIE: I remember this tune. Farm dances.

KATIE: Bananas for the first time.

GERTIE: Your flight lieutenant had a wife and three kids in Bognor.

ELLIE: We only flirted.

KATIE: Harry was my first.

GERTIE: I can see you now: canoodling by the light of tracer bullets, love under the all-clear, oh, I can see it all now.

KATIE: Daft.

GERTIE: We heard all about the ambulance brigade, we heard all about a certain mother of twins shinning up and down ladders into burning houses. Doodle bugs can't keep secrets.

ELLIE: Any Questions hasn't been the same since Freddie Grisewood died.

GERTIE: Gilbert Harding, now there was a rude bugger.

ELLIE: That was Twenty Questions, ignorant.

GERTIE: You better be nice to me or I'll tell about Flight Lieutenant Flopsy.

KATIE: Times have changed. If I learn the guitar, will you two learn?

GERTIE: Me on sitar, Ellie on trombone. We'll call ourselves the Beverley Hillgrannies.

ELLIE: I'm a witch. I can see into the past. I don't like it much, the past, but I can see into it. I can see Gert.

KATIE: What's she doing.

ELLIE: Gertie's got a dirty secret.

GERTIE: She's got us in suspenders again. Come on, Ellie. Spit it out.

ELLIE: In a far-away land a princess gave birth to a monster.

KATIE: Ellie, you alright? Shall I make some more tea, Gert?

GERTIE: She's fine. Come on, Ell. Straight out.

ELLIE I know.

GERTIE: I know you know, you daft cow.

ELLIE You paid for it, of course, no husband, somewhere some strange person —

KATIE: Ellie, I don't think —

GERTIE: You've had a happy life?

ELLIE: I married, I've got a home of my own. I've had everything a woman could want.

KATIE: My house is a bit big, isn't it? I could make the top floor into a flat, maybe let it — Harry and me talked about it. What do you think?

GERTIE: Except babies.

ELLIE: You are an immoral hussy. You always were. Spinster.

KATIE: I never liked gossip.

ELLIE: It was true, wasn't it?

GERTIE: Of course it was.

ELLIE: What was it then, a boy or a girl?

GERTIE: One or the other.

ELLIE: Which?

GERTIE: A girl.

KATIE: Ah.

GERTIE: No — I tell a lie. A boy. Boys have that extra little bit, right?

ELLIE: See.

GERTIE: All sweet, dressed all in blue. Only I never saw him.

KATIE: Was that the year you first went away.

GERTIE: I didn't speak to Mum for two whole years after that. Not a dicky. I shouldn't have listened to her. But I did. Wouldn't want to shock the neighbourhood. She paid my fare, mind.

KATIE: Where did you go?

GERTIE: Poncy Paris. Not exactly a dirty weekend. From his mother's womb untimely ripped, poor little sod.

KATIE: Your own child walking round somewhere.

GERTIE: He probably speaks French like a native.

ELLIE: Whose was it?

GERTIE: Mine.

KATIE: Did you love him?

GERTIE: Don't be daft, I never saw him. Now you see it, now you don't.

ELLIE: I mean, who was it?

GERTIE: You don't really want to know.

ELLIE: You're not going to tell us it was immaculate.

GERTIE: I never loved any man. Like, yes. Some of my best friends are men . . .

ELLIE: Who did it?

KATIE: Shall I make some tea?

GERTIE: You want to know?

ELLIE: Yes.

GERTIE: Fred.

ELLIE: Very funny. See that one coming a mile off.

GERTIE: I told you.

KATIE: Gert —

GERTIE: You may have saved during your engagement, but Fred didn't. He was after everything in skirts in the sound of Bow Bells. He came round to my house once, said he wanted a glass of water. So I thought, right, I'll teach you a lesson, my lad, and I got him in the front room, pushed him on the couch and got his trousers down. Thought that would teach him a lesson but he got the wrong idea and sort of took over. He was in such a hurry to get up and go, he came, so to speak.

ELLIE: You raped him.

GERTIE: You can't rape a man.

ELLIE: As good as.

GERTIE: Not nearly as good as.

ELLIE: How do you know it was him?

GERTIE: He was the only one that summer.

ELLIE: Liar.

GERTIE: Well, I didn't enjoy it, if that makes it better.

ELLIE: But the doctors have all said he's sterile.

GERTIE: There's reasons and reasons for that sort of thing. I must have been the fortunate recipient of the only decent wiggler he could bear to part with.

KATIE: I never believed it.

GERTIE: Everyone else did. No-one said. Mum's the word. I came back all slim and soignee for your wedding, didn't I, Ell?

ELLIE: You're a liar.

GERTIE: I'm not, Ell. I had your son.

Scene Three

Wednesday, a week since the last rehearsal. The third table, ELLIE's table. She and KATIE are having a quick cup of tea, and while they do so they lay a floral embroidered tablecloth on the table, hang some china ducks on the wall. KATIE brings out the hats, now fully decorated with relevant stars etc. A white coat hangs on a peg at the side.

KATIE: Do you think it's alright having plain cloaks? I've got some moons over.

ELLIE: It's Trevor's say-so. How's it going, then?

KATIE: Mustn't grumble. I cleared out the garden shed this week.

ELLIE: What you going to do with all those rooms?

KATIE: I've been thinking about making the top into a flat — you know, to let, maybe.

ELLIE: I wouldn't fancy that at all. Strange people tramping over your head in your own house.

KATIE: They could have their own front door. What do you think?

ELLIE: You might never get them out.

KATIE: Seems daft, just me there.

ELLIE: I like my privacy.

KATIE: You don't have people to stay much, do you?

ELLIE: Spare room's there, just in case. You have to plan.

KATIE: Well, I don't know.

ELLIE: Couldn't you go to live with Jackie, or Jean?

KATIE: I can't, Ell.

ELLIE: I don't know how Gertie's managed all these years; ending up in a room and a cupboard.

KATIE: It's cosy.

ELLIE: And where will she go when the landlord sells it over her head? It happens these days.

KATIE: Gert'll find something. She always does.

ELLIE: We're none of us getting any younger. You've got to bed down proper at our time of life, no good chopping and changing.

KATIE: Are you happy, Ellie?

ELLIE: Happy? I don't bother my head with that.

KATIE *(has noticed the white coat)*: What's this?

ELLIE: That's my lollipop coat.

KATIE: Your what?

ELLIE: I've got a job. White's always suited me.

KATIE: What is it? What do you mean?

ELLIE: Well. You know Fred's leg was playing him up last week, well, on Tuesday he insisted on getting up to collect the pension. Well, he was staggering out the door — won't use a stick — and he bumps into young Dr Robert who's just popping in to see how he is. 'And what have we here,' says Dr Robert. 'You should be in bed, Mr Arbuthnot,' says Dr Robert, and he takes Fred by the arm and nearly carries him back up the stairs — I don't know how he did it, Fred's no feather. Then he comes down and gives me a piece of his mind for letting my ailing husband go out and so on, so I got so annoyed at the both of them I just grabbed my coat and rushed off. I did feel silly, I had to go back for the books, and I had to get Fred to sign his. He was apoplectic, I tell you, but he didn't dare do anything with Dr Robert there.

KATIE: And?

ELLIE: Well. So I get to the post office and I hand over the books and this girl hands over two pensions, and I check it, you can't trust anybody, and I've got less than him. So I says 'I've got less than him, why do I get less than him?' and she says 'Well, madam, you've never paid no stamps, that's why.' 'But I don't eat less than him,' I says. 'I daresay, madam,' she says, 'but we women retire earlier than men, we live longer than men so the money's got to go further and that's why we get less pensions than men.' 'Oh,' I says, 'excuse me, miss, while I go and collect some old ladies and push them under a bus so's there'll be a bit more for you when you retire.'

ELLIE *is shattered; it is the longest speech she has ever made.*

KATIE: Well, I never. So what about the job?

ELLIE: Oh, yes. Well — I saw this poster on the way back. So I'm a lollipop lady now. Fred won't speak to me.

KATIE: How much do you earn?

ELLIE: I didn't ask.

KATIE: You can only earn so much on a pension.

ELLIE: Redcoat Primary, that's where I'll be. I shall invite the polite children home for tea. Look. *(She puts the coat on, pretending to be a lollipop lady.)*

KATIE: I'll cross the road. So will Gert.

ELLIE: Here, don't tell her, will you? I'll surprise her.

KATIE: You know — her kid — if it was you, would you want to meet your child?

ELLIE: No. Best put behind you, that sort of thing.

KATIE: I would. I'd want to know if it looked like me, if it liked me.

ELLIE: She couldn't even remember if it was a boy or a girl.

KATIE: She was kidding.

ELLIE: She never takes anything seriously. You've got to plan your life. Have you made your will?

KATIE: No, no, I haven't.

ELLIE: We have. Well, Fred has.

KATIE: Who you going to leave your lollipop to?

ELLIE: Five more payments and the house is ours. And what's Gertie got?

KATIE: Come on, we don't want to be late.

Scene Four

The same evening. After rehearsal. The canteen table. MEG *is clearing up cups,* GERTIE *is sitting at the table with* Woman's Own, *although she's actually reading a letter.*

MEG: On your tod tonight?

GERTIE: They're watching the costume parade. I had enough.

MEG: Want some tea?

GERTIE: I'll wait for them. *(Pause.)* This your career, then?

MEG: Oh no, it's only evenings. I shall leave in the summer.

GERTIE: And then?

MEG: I'm thinking of going to college.

GERTIE: Well, get you.

MEG: Yes, not bad, eh?

GERTIE: What are you going to study — no, don't tell me. I won't understand it.

MEG: I haven't decided yet. See what A levels I get. I've got other things on my mind.

GERTIE: Eh?

MEG *pats her tummy.*

You ill? What is it, appendix?

MEG: Birds and Bees.

GERTIE: No. How on earth did you manage that?

MEG: Usual way.

GERTIE: See this? *(She taps the letter.)*

MEG: Another French letter?

GERTIE: In a manner of speaking. It's from my son.

MEG: I never knew you were married.

GERTIE: I never was. We made mistakes in my day and all. He's been looking for me for fifteen years. Now. What are you going to do about it?

MEG: I don't know. I suppose I'll have to give up the idea of going to college. I'm not dead certain yet.

GERTIE: Don't let it be adopted.

MEG: I've still got time.

GERTIE: It's never too soon to do your sums. Your boyfriend know?

MEG: No. Anyway, he doesn't care.

GERTIE: Here, my son teaches in a university. Not bad, eh? What about your Mum?

MEG: She'll moan at me — but she's okay, she's great really.

GERTIE: Good for you. Women's lib, eh?

MEG: Rules.

GERTIE: He's coming to London, my son. What do you think — what do you think if we don't like each other.

MEG: Introduce him to me. I like men.

GERTIE: He's old enough to be your father.

MEG: I'll bring Mum round, then. What's his name.

GERTIE: Gerard. Classy French for Gerald, I expect. Lousy name. Still, mothers can't be choosers, eh?

MEG: Better late than never.

    ELLIE *and* KATIE *come in,* KATIE *carrying some sort of velvet or silky dress over one arm.*

MEG *(on her way off to get tea)*: Alright, ladies?

    GERTIE *and* ELLIE *are not talking to each other. Very bristly at first.*

GERTIE: Hello, Kate.

KATIE: Oh, I am tired. All that standing, it's worse than Sainsbury's. Five hundred and fifty-two sequins. *(She holds up the dress.)*

GERTIE: You're a fool to yourself, Katie.

ELLIE: She's looking smug. Cat got the canary?

GERTIE: Grown-up matters. She wouldn't understand.

    ELLIE *has noticed the letter. She is dead curious but has to restrain it as otherwise she would be weakening.* GERTIE *notices her curiosity.*

ELLIE: What's she got there?

GERTIE: I thought she'd never ask.

ELLIE: Another of her stupid games.

KATIE: Oh, pack it in, you two. What is it? Oh, another French postmark. Who's it from?

GERTIE: Guess.

ELLIE: Animal, vegetable or mineral?

GERTIE: A man is all and none of those.

KATIE: Gertie — is it from —

ELLIE: It's Vincent Price looking for a new leading lady.

KATIE: Give it a rest, Ellie.

ELLIE: Not till she apologises.

GERTIE: Real friends don't need to apologise. Tell her.

KATIE: I want to know about the letter.

GERTIE: Real friends discuss what they're going to do with their real friends before they just barge off and do it. Lollipop.

KATIE: Is it from your son?

GERTIE: Our son has found me. Tell her.

KATIE: Now look here. Ellie's apologised, and she said you can cross on her crossing. Alright? Now you start at the beginning, go through to the middle and tell us.

ELLIE: She's just jealous.

GERTIE: Wouldn't be seen dead in that butcher's coat.

KATIE: Oh, you're worse than the twins.

GERTIE: My, my, Katie, you are getting aggressive in your old age.

MEG *arrives with tea.*

GERTIE: Are you sitting comfortably? Well. I got this letter. About a year ago, just after Harry died . . . In French it was, this society, this French society, says my son is trying to trace me and do I wish to be traced?

ELLIE: She doesn't read French. *(KATIE gives her a withering look.)* You don't read French.

GERTIE: Just shows how well you know me. Anyway, maybe I don't want to be traced. So I write back and I say Miss Gertie Hales is very ill in hospital and I'm a very close friend and please tell me more, seeing as how she's seriously ill — anyway. Fifteen years it's taken him.

KATIE: Why did it take him so long?

GERTIE: The nursing home — got bombed or occupied during the war. All the records were gone. Anyway, I liked the way he wrote so I got better quick.

KATIE: Didn't his foster parents know your name?

GERTIE: The nursing home didn't have my real name. I made one up. They only had it in the accounts. Good old Mum.

KATIE: So how — ?

GERTIE: Oh, I don't know all the other details. He spent all those years going round France digging up old nurses. Our frog prince, Ell. Which one of us does he call Mummy?

KATIE: What's his name?

GERTIE *(pronouncing it very French)*: Gerard. Classy, eh? Well, which half do you want, Ell. You can play Solomon *(to KATIE)*.

ELLIE: He'll have to see Fred.

GERTIE: He's well over the age of consent. You'll have to decide, Ellie. His mother the slut or his mother the lollipop?

KATIE: You must feel all funny. What a turn up.

GERTIE: If we don't like each other, I shall simply use it as an opportunity to practise my French.

ELLIE: Natural love's a wonderful thing.

GERTIE: You giving him to me?

KATIE: I don't think you should tell Fred. When are you going to meet him?

GERTIE: He's coming to London. He may be able to come for the play. He's invited me to Paris. Here, Katie, you could come as well.

ELLIE: Fred's the father. He's got his rights.

GERTIE: You know where Fred can stuff his rights, don't you? If he comes to the play, he can come to the first-night party.

KATIE: You'll want to meet him on your own.

GERTIE: I want witnesses. It may be a hoax, a rotten joke by people with a funny sense of humour. Will you come to Paris?

KATIE: I couldn't. I am pleased for you, Gertie.

GERTIE: Not long now. Dress rehearsal tomorrow.

KATIE: Just think, by this time next week it'll be over. I'm ever so nervous.

GERTIE: It'll be alright on the night. Nerves are a good thing.

ELLIE: Fred won't like it.

GERTIE: Fred can bleeding lump it.

KATIE: Come on, Ellie, it's wonderful news.

GERTIE: Look, you've got a lollipop to brighten up your sticky old age, I've got a son. Quits?

KATIE: I can't help being nervous.

GERTIE: I'll walk home with you. Thing about me, Ellie, is underneath I've got a heart of gold. (*To* KATIE.) You're not really going to sew on all them sequins for her?

KATIE: I'll do some. She can finish it.

ELLIE: I don't understand you, Gert.

Scene Five

This scene takes place in KATIE's *house. The space used is the centre of the stage which is empty. The three women come on,* KATIE *perhaps has the cloaks and hats which are now quite finished and decorated. The only piece of furniture used is one of the chairs, to drape the cloaks on.* KATIE *hands out the cloaks. The women put them on, trying the hats, posing a bit,* KATIE *making sure the folds hang well, with the practised eye of a dressmaker.*

ELLIE: Where's it all gone?

KATIE: Sold it. I sold it all.

GERTIE: What, all the furniture?

KATIE: Just the dining room suite. Sideboard, settee, coffee tables. It's always been a dead room.

ELLIE: You going to get something more modern?

KATIE: No.

GERTIE: What, then?

KATIE: Nothing. I don't need it. I haven't used this room for over a year.

ELLIE: It's a nice room.

The cloaks and hats are now all on.

KATIE: There.

GERTIE: Did you hear, Trevor thinks we might do a Restoration comedy next. Lovely clothes they had then.

ELLIE: What you going to do with the money?

KATIE: What money?

ELLIE: From the furniture.

KATIE: I don't know. Gertie can have it for going to Paris. It wasn't much.

GERTIE: Oh no, Katie. Mon fils —

ELLIE: Yer *what*?

GERTIE: Son to you — mon fils is treating me. I shall come back reeking of elegant garlic.

ELLIE: Ugh.

GERTIE: He's coming on Sunday. I shall go back with him on Monday. If I like him.

KATIE: Monday? You never told me.

GERTIE: She never told me about her lollipop, did she?

KATIE: She did. She told you.

ELLIE: What's this Restoration comedy thing?

GERTIE: It's full of very rude people saying and doing very rude things. You won't like it, Ellie.

ELLIE: You mean like Brian Rix?

GERTIE: Something like that.

ELLIE: Then I shall give that one a miss.

KATIE: What, give up the class?

ELLIE: Maybe. I don't know. I told him.

GERTIE: Who? What?

ELLIE: I told Fred about your bastard.

GERTIE: You bleeding never.

ELLIE: Don't worry. I only told him it was yours.

GERTIE: I shall bring him over to your place for tea. That'll be a laugh. Come on, Katie, stop dreaming.

KATIE: Oh yes, mustn't be late. Did you mean that about me going to Paris, Gertie?

GERTIE: Of course I did. I'll check it out for you first, then tell you about it when I get back.

KATIE: Yes. Alright.

ELLIE: Ready?

Scene Six

The following week. The canteen table. ELLIE *and* GERTIE *are at the table.* MEG *is sitting with them.*

MEG: Why did she leave the front door open? Anyone could have walked in.

GERTIE: Anyone didn't. We did.

ELLIE: I just don't understand it, I really don't.

GERTIE: Leave your hanky in your handbag.

MEG: Do you know why?

ELLIE: I've thought and thought. I just don't understand it.

GERTIE: You read the note, didn't you?

ELLIE: Of course I did.

GERTIE: Well, then.

MEG: What did it say?

GERTIE: Read it to her, Ellie. *(She has taken it out of her bag.)* Go on.

ELLIE: I don't want to read it again.

GERTIE: Oh yes you do. Again and again. You read it.

MEG: If it's private —

GERTIE: Suicide's not private. It's everybody's business. Bloody read it, Ellie.

ELLIE: Alright. 'Dear Gertie and Ellie, I'm quite safe now that I can see the walls. I was going to get rid of everything, but I got very tired. So I thought it didn't matter as long as I could see the walls. I'm sorry.'

GERTIE: She's sorry.

ELLIE: 'I'm sorry if this upsets you. You can have my bedside table, Gertie —' Gert, I don't think —

GERTIE: Please.

ELLIE: '— and Ell can have the album. It isn't as if I've got something really bad like cancer, it's just I feel sorry for myself. I never did when Harry was here. I'm alright in the house. I don't have to go out any more.'

GERTIE: Not a dicky about the play.

MEG: Poor old thing.

GERTIE: She wasn't old.

ELLIE: 'I'm sorry. Love, Katie.'

GERTIE: There.

ELLIE: It's one long list when you get to sixty. You just tick things off.

GERTIE: I'm adding things to my list.

ELLIE: You'll die of apoplexy.

GERTIE: Good. Sudden. That's the way. *(Looking upwards.)* Hear that, Missus God? Quick and sudden, alright?

MEG: How did she — ?

GERTIE: Pill bottles everywhere — doors banging, ambulances ringing. What a night. You let that be a lesson to you, my girl.

MEG: How do you mean?

GERTIE: Oh, I don't know. Not to count on her for the first night. I could have told them that. Bloody doctors.

ELLIE: She should have gone to live with Jackie.

GERTIE: And what if she does come back? She might be a bloody vegetable.

MEG: They hadn't sold many tickets, so it didn't matter about putting it off for a week.

GERTIE: Thank you very much.

MEG: You know what I mean.

ELLIE: You can't go to Paris now.

GERTIE: Of course I can't go to Paris now, you silly woman. Can't go to Paris and spend half my day at the Royal General, can I? Bedside table.

ELLIE: I don't understand you.

GERTIE: So you said. *(To Meg.)* You know any witches?

ELLIE: Trevor's got someone. I heard. It feels wrong doing it now, somehow.

GERTIE: It's not wrong. You can mope when there's something to mope about. Suicide's not illegal any more, you know. *(Pause.)* Well, come on, we'd better see who Trevor's got lined up.

MEG: Can anyone go and visit her?

GERTIE: The more the merrier. Here.

MEG: What?

GERTIE: You could do the witch.

MEG: Don't be daft.

GERTIE: You could. She could, couldn't she, Ell?

ELLIE: She's not old enough.

GERTIE: Oh well.

She and ELLIE *get up to go. Then she turns back to* MEG.

If you are expecting, what you do is, you tie a button with four holes in it on a bit of string, then you hold it over your tum. If it swings from right to left, it's a boy, and if it swings from left to right, it's a girl. That way you know what colour to knit.

MEG: Don't be daft, that's an old wives' tale.

ELLIE *(to* MEG*)*: Well, then. We'll see you at the hospital tomorrow?

MEG: Maybe.

WHORES D'OEUVRES

Whores D'Oeuvres was first produced by Omoro Theatre Group, at the Midland Group, Nottingham, on February 8th, 1978, with the following cast:

PAT   Mo Holden
TINA   Rose Waddington

Directed by Malcolm Griffiths

There has been a storm, a freak hurricane. Sound of wind and rain. PAT and TINA are on a makeshift raft, the ripped-away awning of a hotel, moving down the river Thames. PAT wears a policewoman's uniform, very correct, hat, jacket, black stockings and flat shoes. TINA wears casual, comfortable clothes.

On the raft is a broken newsvendor's hut, the magazines all anyhow. PAT is hanging onto it. TINA paces round the edge of the raft, trying to maintain her balance, and attract help, shouting over the sound of the storm.

One   Day – Evening

TINA: Hey — hey — you there —

PAT: Shout louder, you silly bitch, give it all you've got.

TINA: Help — help — over here — Pat, I don't know where we are.

PAT: Don't fucking ask me, yell.

TINA: Hey — someone — we're over here. Oh, it's stupid, there's too much noise.

PAT: Pick up some of that stuff that's floating past — go on —

TINA: What stuff?

PAT: Anything — grab anything — we might need it. Oh, Christ. I'm not a good sailor.

   TINA grabs various objects out of the water; including a broom, a biscuit tin, a white and gilt telephone like Hollywood stars have in their bedrooms.

TINA: Look at this. *(Indicating phone.)*

PAT: Get on with it, for Christ's sake.

TINA: Why don't you bloody come and help?

PAT: Because I'll fall off, that's why.

TINA: Pat — look, there's someone in the water — he's waving — hang on, we're coming.

   She grabs the broom and makes some effort to row.

PAT: We can't control this thing, Tina, we can't jeopardise ourselves for some strange man.

TINA: He's waving.

PAT: Not waving but drowning. Shit. I'm soaked.

TINA: Maybe we'll float all the way to Australia. It's getting calmer, Pat.

PAT: You can row.

TINA: Yes. Sunday afternoons on the Serpentine.

PAT: Why the hell didn't you say?

TINA: You never asked me.

   PAT tries, and finds she can balance upright. She takes her hat off.

   What's the time?

PAT *(shakes her watch)*: Shit. It's bust. Must be after ten.

TINA: What are we going to do, Pat?

PAT: Don't ask me. I didn't know you'd planned an excursion. I thought we were just out for a boring night's leafletting.

TINA: It's getting dark.

PAT: The girl is observant.

TINA: No-one can see us now, can they?

PAT: The girl's an optimist.

TINA: We'll have to stay here, on this thing, all night.

PAT: The girl's a prophet.

TINA: We'll have to sleep here.

PAT: You're a logical genius, Tina.

TINA: Right. We better get organised.

While TINA *tries to right the newsvendor's hut,* PAT *takes off her jacket and skirt, under which she has a shirt and a respectable slip, and folds them carefully.*

TINA: Now what you doing?

PAT: My Mum brought me up to fold my clothes.

TINA: Don't be stupid.

PAT: It's hired, Tina. If I damage it, I got to pay for it, right?

TINA gives up on the hut.

TINA: It's too heavy.

They both sit, dejected.

PAT: Sausages.

TINA: What?

PAT: And eggs. And a bit of fried bread.

TINA: There's a biscuit tin somewhere.

PAT: Open it up, girl, open the box.

TINA *(finds it and holds it for a moment)*: Pat. Betty won't know where I am.

PAT: Nobody knows where you are, Tina.

TINA: It's not funny.

PAT: I thought your Mum was having her for half term?

TINA: She is. But I phone her every morning.

PAT *(indicating Hollywood-type phone)*: There you go. The call's on me.

TINA: Oh, fuck off, Pat.

PAT: It's not my fault. I'm not fucking God. Blame him.

TINA: Drop it.

PAT: Well, open the bloody biscuit tin then. Oh, give it here.

She opens it; there are some biscuits in it.

There. You can thank God now.

TINA: Must be a woman up there, after all.

PAT: We'll be rescued as soon as it's light. Bound to be.

TINA: Sorry I snapped.

PAT: Forget it. Here, we better not finish all the biscuits. What else did you catch?

TINA rummages and finds a transistor radio. She switches it on, and there is just crackling. She switches it off.

TINA: Do you think it's just London? This storm, I mean.

PAT: No idea, love. We better try and sleep.

TINA: We should take turns to stay awake. Just in case.

PAT: I suppose so. *(Indicating the hut.)* Do you think that thing's safe.

TINA: Our temporary erection?

PAT: It's all we'll get tonight. And nothing in the kitty.

They try and adjust to lying down, making a rough pillow with the magazines.

Hang on a minute. *(Yells.)* Here, you fuckers, get your plastic macs and wellies on and come and get it.

Silence.

Right. You got any clean knickers?

TINA: Of course; my Mum always said, you never know when you might be run over.

PAT: Let's have them.

TINA: We can't share one pair of knickers.

PAT: I only want to borrow them.

TINA gets a spare pair out of a pocket, and watches, while PAT hangs it on the edge of the hut.

Keep the tigers away.

TINA: I wish I was at home.

PAT: I wish I was reclining on the back seat of my Silver Cloud, flanked by my Tibetan sheep-dogs, my Amazon chauffeur in her leopard-skin bikini feeding me champagne as she languorously massages my languid body.

TINA: I didn't understand a word of that.

PAT: Put it down to my happy childhood.

TINA: You got a vivid imagination.

PAT: Or something. *(She rifles through the magazines.)* A little bedtime reading for madam? Cosmo, Playhouse, Penthouse, Whitehouse — no, Mary's not in that one this time.

TINA: Let's have a look. Here, that's Jill. It's Jill in that one.

PAT: So it is. Wonder how much she got for that.

TINA: She's called 'Ariana' in here. Hobbies: painting, sailing, good food and relaxing. In between spells in Holloway.

PAT: It doesn't say that, does it?

TINA: No. I just said it. *(She yawns.)*

PAT: You sleep first.

TINA: Here.

PAT: Now what?

TINA: Nothing. Just wondered whether I turned the gas off.

PAT: Goodnight.

TINA: What you gonna do? Read a magazine?

PAT: No. I just look at the pretty pictures. Ariana, eh.

Two   Night – Dream

Episode One

TINA *has just arrived in the big city. She stands nervously waiting.* PAT *walks casually past, turns and walks back.*

PAT: Just arrived, love?

TINA: Yes.

PAT: Waiting for someone?

TINA: Yes.

PAT: Friend?

TINA: Yes.

PAT: Late, is she?

TINA: Yes. A bit.

    Pause.

PAT: Looks like she's not coming, doesn't it?

TINA: I don't know.

PAT: Got a phone number for her?

TINA: Yes.

PAT: Like me to ring her for you? Then you won't miss her if she turns up.

TINA: Oh, thank you.

    PAT *moves off to one side and does nothing.*

PAT: No answer there, darling. Looks like she's not bothering.

TINA: Oh.

PAT: You got anyone else here — cousin, or something?

TINA: No-one.

PAT: I'll tell you what I'll do. My sister runs this little hotel, just round the back of the station — she may be able to put you up — just as a favour to me, mind.

TINA: That's very kind of you —

PAT: We can't have a nice young girl walking the streets, now, can we? You got any money?

TINA: Only a few quid.

PAT: There you are, then. You'll need that till you get set up. Got a job?

TINA: Not yet.

PAT: Well, we might be able to fix you up, then.

TINA: I haven't really got any qualifications —

PAT: We'll find you some of those as well, eh? Just left school, have you?

Episode Two

TINA *is now standing around on the street, waiting for a punter.* PAT *comes past in a car, kerb-crawling.*

PAT: 'Evening, love.

TINA: 'Evening.

PAT: Looking for company?

TINA: Maybe.

PAT: How much company?

TINA: You tell me.

PAT: Fiver?

TINA: What for?

PAT: Quick one in the back of the car?

TINA: Tenner.

PAT: Give me an extra special little ride?

TINA: It *is* coming on to rain, isn't it?

Episode Three

TINA *lounges nonchalantly, looking at her watch as though waiting for someone.*

PAT: Waiting for someone?

TINA: Maybe.

PAT: A friend?

TINA: Maybe.

PAT: You wouldn't be committing an offence, by any chance, would you?

TINA: What, me?

PAT: Yes, you. You do know that the Queen's most Excellent Majesty, and a whole lot of other people, have declared that it is an offence for a common prostitute to loiter or solicit in a street or public place for the purpose of prostitution.

TINA: A common prostitute? Well, I never.

PAT: Oh, I'm sure you have. I think you'd better come along with me.

TINA: My friend must have let me down. You can't trust anyone nowadays, can you, officer? Oh, well, be seeing you. *(And she goes to move off.* PAT *stops her.)*

PAT: Now just one moment, young lady. You stand right here while I'm talking to you.

TINA: Are you suggesting that I should loiter, officer?

PAT: Now don't you come it with me, young lady. One word from me —

TINA: Oh, yes? What word is that, then?

PAT: No fucking lip from you, my girl.

TINA: Well, get out of my way and let me get on about my business.

PAT: You think you can fool me, don't you? Well, I think you'd better come down to the cop shop and have a few words with the other lads, that's what I think.

TINA: All right, all right, no need to break my fucking arm.

PAT: Language, young lady.

TINA: I'm not your bleeding young lady.

PAT: I'll say.

TINA: I could be.

PAT: Oh yes?

TINA: Oh yes. Lighten the path of duty.

PAT: You wouldn't be trying to solicit me, would you?

TINA: Perish the thought, officer.

PAT: Perish indeed.

TINA: You don't really want to waste a whole day in court on little me, do you, Mr Policeman, sir?

PAT: I don't think I'm at liberty to discuss that with the accused.

TINA: Why, you could be sitting back at the station, looking through all those magazines with pretty coloured pictures, from those little shops you like so much.

PAT: My reading habits are my own affair.

TINA: Fancy a quick French lesson?

PAT: Not much call for French round these parts.

TINA: Want to buy a large chest of drawers?

PAT: Not just at the moment, thank you.

TINA: Nice bit of English conversation?

PAT: Ah, now you're talking.

TINA *and* PAT *move off.*

TINA: Normally I'd charge — oh, ever so much — but for you . . .

Three   Day – Morning

The raft is fairly tidy. PAT *is trying to tune the radio.* TINA *is steering with the broom.*

PAT: Recognise the landscape?

TINA: Don't know. Level with Herne Bay, maybe. Kent, perhaps. Depends how far we drifted in the night.

PAT: Couldn't we land or something? No-one can see us out here.

TINA: They could see us from the cliffs

PAT: But they might think we're a holiday boat or something.

TINA: There's been nothing but ruined houses all the way. We're better off moving till we find somewhere likely.

   PAT *has got something on the radio.*

NEWSCASTER: . . . large parts of South-East England have been devastated by the freak storm. The river Thames has broken through its flood barriers, and so far twenty people have been drowned. Damage to property is estimated — *(*PAT *switches it off.)*

TINA: Leave it on.

PAT: Save the batteries.

TINA: Well, hello there, Hurricane Pat.

PAT: Wotcha, Typhoon Tina.

TINA: They're not allowed to do that any more. Blame women for freaks of nature. They have to alternate Hurricane Pat with Hurricane Peter. In America, anyway.

PAT: You're very well up on the weather.

TINA: Read it in the *Mirror*. Or was it the *Sun*?

PAT: We'll be alright once the Navy gets here.

TINA: We're going in — there's a bay.

   The raft touches land; the two jump off, and sway for a moment while they find their land legs. They go off in opposite directions to look for a path. PAT *disappears briefly from view, then the two meet again,* PAT *carrying a picnic basket, a teddy-bear and a skateboard.*

TINA: There's no way up.

PAT: There is.

TINA: Where?

PAT: Over there. *(*TINA *starts going in that direction.)* It's blocked. Cliff's fallen down.

TINA: What have you got there?

PAT: Special treat.

   She opens the basket. There is food in it.

   Come on. Get stuck in. Don't look a gift horse.

TINA: Where has all this come from?

PAT: Birthday present.

TINA: What do you mean?

PAT: Got caught short.

TINA: I'm going to have a look.

PAT: I shouldn't. It's not a pretty sight.

TINA: I'm going.

PAT: Four of them. Dead. I think it's four. You can't see much under the rocks.

TINA: Oh, Christ.

PAT: Landslide, I think. Come on. The food's fresh. I reckon they may have been looking for crabs. The food was by the boat.

TINA: Boat?

PAT: Smithereens. Splinters. Make a good fire, but no good for the sea unless you don't mind getting your feet wet.

TINA: Oh, God.

PAT: Ever had crabs? Nasty, itchy things.

TINA: Give over, Pat.

PAT: Come on, love. Get some food down you. The bodies aren't even smelly yet. Anyway, they're down wind of us.

TINA: I'm not hungry.

PAT: You're still alive. Get on with it. *(TINA begins to eat.)*

TINA: I don't think I'll look at them.

PAT: That's the ticket.

TINA: Didn't it make you feel ill?

PAT: Being a nurse cures all that. Kills or cures.

TINA: Did you like being a nurse?

PAT: It was alright. Taught me how bits of the body work. Or don't. I've found that very handy. Demolition expert on temporary erections, that's me. I should have gone into the building trade.

TINA: I wanted to be a nurse.

PAT: No fucking future in that.

TINA: Here, do you think they'll have anything about us on the news?

PAT: Sure to. Tidal Wave Hits Central London. Havoc at Whores Haven. I used to work that hotel, you know. Year or two back. Before I met you. Then they got a new maitre d'. Pain in the arse. He threw me out, the bugger. Never thought I'd be sailing the sea on the bloody awning.

TINA: We could sell our story to the papers when we get back. Make a fortune, eh? Two plucky tarts survive on a raft, with a thermos of tea and a pile of leaflets to organise other fallen ladies.

PAT: Here, that's a thought. We got to name our brave craft.

TINA: The Cuntiki?

PAT: No. It's got to have class. How about — the Margaret Thatcher?

TINA: Ugh.

PAT: Steer us into calm, well-spoken waters. No? No. Then — the Josephine Butler.

TINA: Never heard of her.

PAT: Fiona Richmond, patron saint of the Porn Squad.

TINA: Princess Anne? Charlie's Aunt?

PAT: Who's that?

TINA: Princess Margaret.

PAT: No. It'll have to be the Josephine Butler.

TINA: Are you quite sure about that, Patricia Harris?

PAT: Oh, quite, quite sure, miss.

TINA: And who was this Josephine Butler?

PAT: Never heard of her, miss. I made her up.

TINA: Well, I shall tell you. *(She takes a stick.)* Now then. Our subject today is C.D.

PAT: Hernia today, gonorrhea tomorrow.

TINA: C.D., Patricia Harris, not V.D. Contagious Diseases, as any whore worth her salt knows. Now, let us look at the army —

PAT: — and the Navy and the Airforce and —

TINA: A fighting army marches on its — let me put it another way. A soldier must be well trained, fit and happy. He must play as well as work. He must have his little tot of rum and his loose lady and with a little bit of bad luck the loose lady will end up with the little tot.

PAT: Get 'em off, miss.

TINA: I shall send you to the headmaster, Patricia Harris.

PAT: Promises, promises.

TINA: Now over a hundred years ago, many of our brave soldiers and sailors were being sabotaged. A lot of very bad ladies gave them a touch of the creepy-crawlies in their lower decks. And very itchy they are too.

PAT: Ooh.

TINA: Now the good Parliament of the day, rightly full of good men, upright (well, sometimes) and true, passed an Act that said that all these wicked women must be examined for filthy disease, and go to the good hospital if they were so found, and any filthy women that refused could be sent to prison.

PAT: Was this Josephine Butler a filthy woman, miss?

TINA: You silly little bitch, she was a woman who helped repeal those idiot Acts, and a long time it took too, and a good thing, because without her, my young lovely, you and me might be stuck in the clink good and proper.

TINA *wields the stick threateningly and over the next section begins to flagellate* PAT *who enters into the spirit of the game they both know they are playing.*

PAT: But we are, miss.

TINA: So we are, so we are. And why is that?

PAT: Because we are wicked and corrupt.

TINA: What are we?

PAT: Evil, leading innocent men on and then taking their money from them.

TINA: Oh, no, we're not.

PAT: Oh, yes we are.

TINA: When do we take their money?

PAT: When they come with us.

TINA: When they *what*?

PAT: When they come —

TINA: Dirty girl.

PAT: Please don't hit me, Madam.

TINA: You are my servant, and a wicked girl, and servants may not have followers. What may you not have?

PAT: Followers, Madam.

TINA: And you let your young man come in here —

PAT: Yes, I let my young man come.

TINA: You slut, dirty, wicked, filthy slut; strumpet, harlot, hussy, minx, trollop, tart — *whore*.

PAT: More, give me more, the whore wants more.

TINA: Oh, this chastisement is such hard work, I am quite wore out.

PAT: Oh, Madam, let me do it for you. *(She takes the stick and hits herself.)*

TINA: That's quite enough of that — now off upstairs with you and service the master.

They both collapse into giggles and then lie back, quite wore out. TINA *begins to try the radio again. We hear, loud and clear, the signature tune of Desert Island Discs. To the tune of this* PAT *takes her contraceptive pill, gives one to* TINA, *takes one herself and then the two of them each drop their pill in the other's mouth à la 'Beulah, peel me a grape'.*

Four   Night – Dream

PAT *lies as though sleeping;* TINA *is on the skateboard (or a single skate if this proves difficult) moving round and round* PAT, *goading her to wake up.* TINA, *in Episode One, is a ponce.*

Episode One

TINA: Daisy, daisy, give me your tits to chew
    I'm half crazy, me balls are turning blue
    I can't afford a johnny, a plastic bag will do
    But you look sweet upon a sheet with me on top of you

Come on, girlie, lazy daisy, rise and shine, give us a rise, shine your nose, give me this day my daily bread and get the fuck on with it.

PAT *wakes, moves dejectedly under the pole that has the 'Josephine B' knickers on it.*

Not like that, baby, don't look so miserable, lift your tits and hoick your eyelashes, you'll be saying next you don't enjoy your work.

PAT: I don't.

TINA: Bit of lip, there, eh? Want to *enjoy* it? I got news for you, darling, you're the ultimate in alienation, right? You're it with a capital A. You want the impossible, don't you? A whore, *feel*?

During this next short sequence, for the first three letters PAT *goes into a series of porny letter poses, and then for the last three, while she is calling the letters,* TINA *joins her, till by the end the two of them are in the kind of poses that Vogue and the classier magazines go in for.*

Give us an S
give us an E
give us an X
give us a P
give us an O
give us a T

and what have we got? SEXPOT.

TINA *breaks from the pose and resumes her directorial role.*

Much better, sweetie, now let's take it from the top and we'll have a touch of the Julie Christies this time round — give us an S —

PAT *repeats her poses alone.*

PAT: Come you spirits,
         That tend on mortal thoughts, unsex me here,
         And fill me from the crown to the toe, top-full
         Of direst cruelty:

TINA: Give us an E, pout and thrust, ashes to ashes and money in the bank, now go to it like the flies on the wall and give us an X once more with feeling —

PAT: make thick my blood
         Stop up th'access and passage to remorse,
         That no compunctious visitings of Nature
         Shake my fell purpose, nor keep peace between
         Th'effect and it.

TINA: Keep your feet clean and your mouth shut, give us a P, a touch of the Monroes, keep the streets clean and look at the legs on that one, so give us an O, what the eye doesn't see the morality won't grieve over, for God's sake give us the big O —

PAT: Come to my woman's breasts,
         And take my milk for gall, you murth'ring ministers —

TINA: Passion, even, well, you won't need that, my darling, come on, you can make poetry sound like dirt, come on then, slack, it suits you to a T, give us a T — or you'll feel the back of my whip where it doesn't show when you're flat on your back. Come on, then, show me —

Episode Two

PAT *now does a come-on to* TINA *which at first is coy and feminine and then grows in forcefulness until the positions become reversed, and* PAT *is so aggressive that her behaviour, being like that of a man, puts* TINA *into a female role — and the roles are now reversed from Episode One.*

TINA *is now leading a voracious* PAT *back to* TINA's *pad, trying to keep* PAT's *pawing to a minimum.* PAT *is the male customer.*

TINA: Drinkie?

   PAT *makes as though knocking the glass out of her hand.*

   Well, we are impatient, aren't we, duckie?

PAT: How much?

TINA: What you in?

PAT: Oil.

TINA: Olive or petroleum?

PAT: What's that to you?

TINA: Supply and demand. I charge according to the need.

PAT: Persian Gulf.

TINA: Fifty.

PAT: For the whole night?

TINA: Seventy-five.

PAT: Anything I want? Any way I want it?

TINA: Seventy-five for a straight night. Any extras is extra.

PAT: I'm hungry and my shoes need polishing, change my nappy and let me lick you out.

TINA: All bloody right, then.

PAT: Now.

TINA: You wait till I'm good and ready, sweetie, alright?

   PAT *flings* TINA *down on her back, legs spread-eagled (no nudity in this play, remember).* PAT *stands over her, taking money out of her pocket.*

PAT: Hungry, darling? Want your dinner? Fish and chips? Nice bit of fish for pussy? How would you like it? Fivers? Ten bob notes? Oh, I forgot, we don't have them no more, do we, it'll have to be 50p pieces, won't it, nice straight edges, you can have it all in 50p pieces, right where you want it.

   PAT *simulates shoving money up* TINA's *cunt.* TINA *at first reacts as though this is just another gig, but it becomes painful, and she writhes in agony. She simulates as though her arms and legs are tied spread-eagled, though* PAT *hasn't literally tied her.*

   Just what you want, eh? It'll be a bit messy, but a quick soak in biological detergent and the bank won't know the difference from mint condition. Can't get enough of it, eh? If you're very good and ask me very very nicely I'll ram my beautiful big cock up you as well, and there's no use your saying no because I know you mean yes, don't I?

PAT *stands quite still while* TINA *simulates being raped. She screams and then lies there still and silent.* PAT *throws a five-pound note on her and then we move into —*

Episode Three

PAT, *either still standing over her or having moved to pick up the note, is now the ponce.*

PAT: Fuckin' fiver. A whole night and all she's got to show is a fiver. Who does she think she's kidding? Where have you hidden the rest of it? Think you can shove it all up yourself and no-one will know —

And PAT *is kicking* TINA, *who finally screams and breaks free to go back to where she was sleeping and sit there in a terrified huddle.*

Five   Day – Morning

TINA *is still sitting in the position she was in at the end of the last scene,* PAT *is clearing things up, preparing the raft ready to move off. She occasionally casts a concerned glance across at* TINA. *She finishes the preparations.*

PAT: Ready, then.

TINA *is silent.*

PAT: You can't just sit there. Come on, let's get going.

TINA *(starts moving slowly)*:   Yes.

PAT: Fancy a swim?

TINA: It's too cold.

PAT *tries the radio. Crackle. No clear sound.*

TINA: The batteries are fucked.

PAT: That's more than I can say for us.

TINA: Drop it, for shit's sake.

PAT: Eh?

TINA: You're always on about sex.

PAT: Sex? Shop talk, love, gossip of the trade.

TINA: Well, I don't want to hear it.

PAT: You have got up on the wrong side of the beach, haven't you?

TINA: Come on.

PAT: Has madam had enough breakfast? Cornflakes, champagne, smoked salmon and cream cheese?

TINA: Is that what you get when you do the diplomats' run?

PAT: Depends where I stay.

TINA: You're all right then, aren't you?

PAT: I think we'd better get rescued soon.

They are on the raft now and set sail. TINA *is steering with the broom, while* PAT *sets up a fishing line with a piece of string and a bent safety pin.*

PAT: They say a man can go for five days without water.

TINA: If a man can, we can.

PAT: You should have had some of that tea. You'll get dehydrated.

TINA: I'll bloody have it later.

PAT: No swearing in front of the tiddlers.

Silence.

TINA: Betty likes fishing.

PAT: She's bound to be okay, Tina.

TINA: You don't know what it's like to have a kid.

PAT: True. Very true.

TINA: Won't George be worried?

PAT: No. George knows I can take care of myself.

TINA: He'll think you've just tripped off on a long weekend with the House of Lords.

PAT: Maybe.

TINA: You do all right really, don't you?

PAT: Of course, I'm a professional. Here, you're good at this steering.

TINA: I mean, you're all safe and set up, aren't you?

PAT: I saw this tele programme about a woman who sailed round the world, all on her tod. Storms, misery, the lot.

TINA: You must make as much as the Director-General of the BBC.

PAT: She must be really tough.

TINA: Why do you bother organising other whores? You're okay.

PAT: I bet she'll settle down in the end. You can't sail round the world with a husband and family.

TINA: I think you're doing it because you feel guilty about something.

PAT: Maybe you can, though.

TINA: It doesn't really make any difference to you whether the police leave us alone or not. You don't work the streets. You don't get arrested.

PAT: What's your Betty want to be when she grows up?

TINA: She's not following in her mother's footsteps, that's for sure.

PAT: How are you going to explain to her what you do?

TINA: I won't tell her.

PAT: Pull the other one. She's not stupid.

TINA: I'm going to get out of it.

PAT: And who's going to pay the rent?

TINA: I don't know.

PAT: Well, that's why I bloody organise. Because I want you to be able to pay your rent.

TINA: Since when are you running a soup kitchen?

PAT: You jealous?

TINA: Maybe.

PAT: I'm a pro, I told you. I take a pride in my work.

TINA: It's all right for you at the top end of the market.

PAT: Don't you kid yourself. I spend a fortune on nail polish. I have to read the bloody *Times* and the *New Statesman* to keep up.

TINA: It's just a joke to you, isn't it?

PAT: They used to burn whores. They never burned the men, mind.

TINA: Why don't you get a job?

PAT: My punters pay a fair price and they know how to treat a woman.

TINA: We can't all do escort agency work.

PAT: There you are — you've got no ambition. Anyone can get to the top now if they really want to. We've all got our preconditions now.

TINA: Our what?

PAT: Preconditions for prostitution with a smile. Home is the sailor, home from the sea, and the prostitute's on the pill. If more women took the pill they wouldn't be so bothered about rape.

TINA: Helen got her face slashed last week.

PAT: I weep with one eye and laugh with the other.

TINA: She comes from a really classy family. Her mum was a debutante.

PAT: Yes, well, it pays to have a good family behind you. You can always go off into the country when things go bad.

TINA: They say the pill puts you off sex.

PAT: All the better then. You can just look on it as a job.

TINA: It's sex for the men.

PAT: That's their problem, then, isn't it?

TINA: I mean, don't you ever think about other women?

PAT: Yes. Other women are fools.

TINA: I'm not doing it for the money.

PAT: Tart with a heart of gold?

TINA: Well — I mean, it *is* for the money —

PAT: Look, it's a job. If we could get better jobs we wouldn't do it. Get the police off our backs. That's all we want.

TINA: I don't know.

PAT: Yes, you do. You've come leafletting three weekends. You know.

TINA: I hate it.

PAT: Yes, well.

TINA: I mean, it isn't — satisfactory, is it?

PAT: There's not much that is for a woman.

TINA: I hate it. Every time. I keep thinking it won't matter. But it does. I hate them. I hate myself. Don't you?

PAT: The only way out of this game is feet first.

TINA: But don't you?

PAT: Men are nothing. They need us more than we need them. Women don't need men in bed any more than we need them anywhere else.

TINA: But you can't go on for ever, Pat.

PAT: When I retire I shall go into business. Run a flat, ex-directory phone number. Madame Patricia's high-class companions for all occasions. Never know — there might be a slot for you.

TINA: Barclay Card, Access, American Express accepted.

PAT: Yes, why not? There's not enough enterprise in this country. I reckon we have to stimulate the small man to achieve a better performance, increase production, right?

TINA: Supply and demand.

PAT: Society has its itch and we scratch it.

TINA: Foreign currency, package tours. Do you love George?

PAT: I make him cup-a-soup when he's ill.

TINA: What if he went to a whore?

PAT: He does. Me.

TINA: I mean someone else.

PAT: Do me a favour.

TINA: Like, say it was me. You know. No hassles. Straight, regular deal.

PAT: He wouldn't, love.

TINA: Why not?

PAT: Take it from me, love.

TINA: But what if he did? Would he tell you?

PAT: What do you think we are, married or something?

TINA: No.

PAT: He's not my ponce, you know. He's just got a working common law wife, that's all.

TINA: But if?

PAT: He, er, he has a little trouble getting interested.

TINA: I didn't know that.

PAT: Well, it just slipped out.

TINA: So to speak.

PAT: Yes.

TINA: He can, you know.

PAT: He thinks getting whores organised is a great idea. He thinks that once we're accepted and the bloody state leaves us alone, society will be a much healthier place. We should occupy the churches like they did in France.

TINA: It hasn't done them much good.

PAT: Yes, well, society's got to recognise that we provide a necessary service.

TINA: Sort of — therapy?

PAT: If you like.

TINA: He's going with Jamie.

PAT: Straighten out their hypocrisy. Any shop can sell this muck *(referring to girlie mags)*, a quick fine and they're back on the job. Knocking shops isn't in it.

TINA: Jamie told me.

PAT: Jamie's a pimp and a queer.

TINA: And we're a couple of whores.

PAT: I don't believe you.

TINA: But if?

PAT: I'd sling him out on his ear.

TINA: But why?

PAT: I just would. It's my business. He's my bloke.

Six Night – Dream

PAT *and* TINA *are asleep. They are at opposite ends of the raft. A contrast to their first night when they were cosy together.*

Episode One

TINA *wakes and sits up.*

TINA: Do not prostitute thy daughter, nor cause her to be a whore; lest the land fall to whoredom and the land become full of wickedness.

Pause.

PAT *wakes and sits up.*

PAT: He that is without sin among you, let him first cast a stone at her.

Pause.

A telephone rings shrilly, once. PAT *rises and moves. She is a hustler answering the phone.*

PAT: Hello, soldier.

The telephone rings shrilly, once. TINA *rises and moves. She is a wife being phoned by her husband.*

TINA: Hello, darling.

PAT: Yes. Yes, that's me. Strict discipline. Where are you from, soldier? Oh, I do beg your pardon, a Member of Parliament. *(Clearly she does not believe this.)* Can I call you 'Member' for short? Or 'Member' for long? Just my little joke.

TINA: Yes. Yes. Oh. How late?

PAT: Why, of course. Let me see. I'm five foot seven. I have legs going up to my shoulders, v-e-r-y slim ankles, tits so snowy you could sing Christmas carols under them — why, no, of course I don't kiss — I wouldn't want you to catch anything, now, would I? No, I don't mind where I do it. On the floor — in a churchyard? Why, yes among the dead, in the middle of the slime, slime to slime, you and me —

TINA *(shouts)*: I won't wait up.

Episode Two

TINA: dip dip dip
         my little ship
         sails on the water
         like a cup and saucer
         W-H-O-R-E spells 'Out'.

PAT: Come and join us, scab. Wifey.

TINA: Why do you have to hate me?

PAT: Blackleg. Undercut the rates, cross the picket line. Scab.

TINA: Why?

PAT: Married ladies of the land. Permissive liberated women. Philanthropists, the cowardly lot of you. You relieve that itch for free.

TINA: What do you want?

PAT: We'll picket outside your bedroom window. If you can't wave a five-pound note outside by two a.m. at the very latest, you'll be a scab and a blackleg and we'll break in and kneecap you.

TINA: I love him.

PAT: Love. In this goddam society.

TINA: How can you live without it?

PAT: Love's not my business, baby, keeping the punters satisfied is. The difference between me and you is that I keep my bargain and you don't.

TINA: Thief.

PAT: Confidence trickster. You want his wage packet and his prick and nothing in return. Whore.

TINA: You're the whore.

PAT: I'm not afraid of the truth.

TINA: Your face is wet. Salty. Is it tears? Sweat?

PAT: I didn't fucking choose it, but I'm happy with it.

TINA: I can make you redundant.

PAT: It's the oldest profession.

TINA: We'll all make you redundant.

PAT: You and whose revolutionary party?

TINA: There's enough of us think you're wrong.

PAT: Go to work on an orgasm? Out of sight, out of mind, that's you. Scrub the dirty scrubbers away under the mat, hide the outcasts, keep your high heels smooth and shining, step over us carefully in case you slip in our filth. And thank you, ma'am, three bags full, clean your filth for you.

TINA: Pride in your work?

PAT: Pride in our work.

TINA: A private act between consenting adults.

PAT: That's right. No offence to anyone.

TINA: Just because you're behind closed doors doesn't mean you don't affect anyone.

PAT: Pride in our work.

TINA: So pay your union dues, have your lobotomy on the National Health, reduce yourself to the cash nexus.

PAT: If cash nexus is posh for cunt, then you're spot on. They'll sell my body without asking me — I'll do it myself, my way.

TINA: You're not happy with that.

PAT: All women are prostitutes. Some are more common than others.

TINA: Try telling them that.

PAT: I am, kid, but it doesn't seem to get through.

TINA: There's millions of them who don't earn enough, thousands of women not happy with their lives, but they don't go on the game. Why?

PAT: Because they're stupid. You walk round with a fortune between your legs, that's the way to get the money back from the men who've stolen it from us.

TINA: You smell of hate.

PAT: And you stink of cowardice and guilt. You can't do it, can you? Fishnet tights, high heels, suspenders, black velvet cut high over your thighs? White powder puff on your bum? You daren't.

TINA: I don't hate myself that much.

PAT: You've got the world the wrong way up. You have your security because of me.

TINA: You need me for your image.

PAT: Don't make me laugh.

TINA: State brothels, call-girl matrons, free red-light bulbs from the local council, surgery hours.

PAT: I'm no sodding socialist.

TINA: Well, we know where we stand then, don't we?

PAT: We do.

TINA: Well, get it together. Get right in or stay right out.

PAT: You should have been a policewoman.

TINA: You've got one for your shadow.

PAT: dip dip dip
        my little ship
        sails on the water
        like a cup and saucer
        O-U-T spells 'Whore'.

TINA: You'll want to be paid for your fucking dreams next.

Seven   Day – Next Morning

PAT *and* TINA *are roughly in the same positions they were in at the end of Scene 5. There is a coolness between them to start with. A slightly mechanical feeling; they are both tired and thirsty.* TINA *is steering.* PAT *is trying the radio but getting only very faint static.*

TINA: It's no use, it's bloody useless.

PAT: We should try and land. At least we can find some water.

TINA: Betty will think I'm dead.

PAT: So she'll get a pleasant surprise, won't she?

TINA: What makes you so sure?

PAT: I'm not sure. I brought me stiff upper lip in me bag. I'm going to put my trust in the British Navy. Betty could join the force.

TINA: She'll decide for herself.

PAT: Of course she will. I'm only passing the time.

TINA: Look, Pat — round there, past that rock, can you see?

PAT: It's a bloody mirage. It's all misty.

TINA: It's a boat, I'm sure it's a boat.

    PAT *puts on her policewoman's skirt, hat and jacket during this next section.*

PAT: I told you.

TINA: For God's sake look — can you see it?

PAT: Bloody mad idea, hiring a policewoman's uniform so we wouldn't get arrested for soliciting or obstruction. How naive can you get?

TINA: It's not a boat — it looks like a pier.

PAT: Southend.

TINA: Don't be stupid, we're nowhere near Southend.

PAT: I mean, who's going to believe a policewoman giving out leaflets to make prostitution respectable?

TINA: Will you stop muttering and row?

PAT: It is a boat, it's a boat next to the pier. I knew the Navy wouldn't let us down.

TINA: You steer.

    TINA *hands over the broom while she collects her bag, etc. She finds a pile of leaflets and is just throwing them away — overboard —*

PAT: Hey, what are you doing?

TINA: We won't need those.

PAT: That lot cost ten quid.

TINA: Well, I'm getting out.

PAT: Not till we land you're not.

TINA: I've decided. I'm going on the dole when we get back.

PAT: Oh yes? Mr Social Services going to pay your rent?

TINA: I'll borrow.

PAT: You'll be back on the game inside a week.

TINA: We'll see.

PAT: What you need is a good night's sleep, get back to normal.

TINA: I mean it, Pat.

PAT: You're dehydrated.

TINA: You should get out.

PAT: Don't you moralise me.

TINA: I'm not. You're not really happy, are you?

PAT: Nor will you be, explaining what you've been living on for the last God knows how long. It's not much of a qualification for work.

TINA: You're right. It is the Navy.

PAT: Look at their little pips. They've got a rope.

A rope is thrown on. They catch it and secure it round an end as the raft is drawn to the boat or pier.

TINA: I mean it. I have decided. There's no future in it. Not even for you, Pat.

PAT: Seeing's believing.

TINA: You'll see.

PAT: You got some real-life lover on the side who can see right up you into your heart of gold?

TINA: No. Just Betty and me.

PAT: And good luck to all who sail in her.

TINA *has the end of the rope now and she jumps off the raft, out of our sight, calling from offstage.*

TINA: Come on, Pat, give us your hand.

PAT *(looks round for a moment, straightens her uniform while she says or sings softly)*: where the bee sucks
there suck I
in the fallen bed
there I lie.

A final twitch to her uniform, a wave to the lads off, and —

PAT: I've always liked a nice uniform.

And she too jumps off the raft, offstage as the music swells to a rousing chorus of 'What shall we do with a drunken sailor?'

SCISSORS

Scissors was first performed at the Almost Free Theatre in London, on April 2nd, 1978, with the following cast:

JOSHUA	Allan Corduner
GERRY	Neil Gibson
NORMA	Lesley Joseph
MIRIAM	Barbara Lott
MAX	Jack Lynn

Directed by Nicholas Barter
Designed by Norman Coates
Stage Manager, Ross Foley
Lighting by Peter Southcott

A living-room in a North-East London terrace house. A TV, a small couch, a sideboard with a menorah and a pair of medium-sized tailor's scissors on it, two or three reels of cotton, needles and a box of pins. In one corner of the room is an old-fashioned tailor's dummy, on which there is a half-finished tweed jacket. One sleeve is basted in, the other is thrown across the shoulder. The hem is still unfinished, and there are no button-holes. Near the stand are a wooden yardstick and a tape measure. On the window sill are a few tomato plants in pots. There is a table and four chairs. A radio is on the table.

Scene One   Wednesday afternoon

MAX *is sitting on the couch, watching the end of a TV wrestling programme.*

MAX: Look at that mad sod. He'll kill him. Go on, kill him. Ah, that's illegal, give him a public warning — yes, another power driver, go on — he's got him, Miri, you should see this, two super-heavyweights — oh, they're horrible —

MIRIAM *(off)*: Have you got your shoes on?

MAX *(grabbing the shoes which are beside him and putting them on)*: What?

COMPERE *(from TV)*: Seconds away. Round two.

MAX: He's thrown him out of the ring — first thing, he throws him out of the ring, he's walking off —

MIRIAM *(off)*: I said, have you got your shoes on?

COMPERE: He's angry, he's really angry now.

MAX: Look, the madman, twenty-five stone — oy veh, they got the referee between them — thirty stone the other side — they got the St John's Ambulance Brigade coming in, oh, the poor bastard, he's squashed between them — they're taking the referee off on a stretcher.

COMPERE: This contest will have to be abandoned.

Roar of protest from the TV; MAX switches it off in disgust. He notices a fly buzzing, swats at it with a newspaper, and it falls dead. He stands over it.

MAX: One, two, three, four, five, six . . .

As he counts it out, NORMA appears in the doorway, holding an evening paper.

MIRIAM *(off)*: Switch that rubbish off already.

MAX: — seven, eight, nine, ten — *(He looks up and sees NORMA.)* It was laying on its back so I counted it out. You want I should say Kaddish for it as well?

NORMA: Poor little fly.

MAX: Poor little fly, she says. You drive all the way from sunny Brighton, and you don't kiss your father hello?

NORMA *(kisses him)*: You've been eating garlic.

MAX: Aftershave.

NORMA: Garlic aftershave?

MAX: So take your coat off. Unpack. Did you put your car round the corner? Where's the luggage?

NORMA: I left my bag in the car. Mum said we were going to have tea with Auntie Ada.

MIRIAM *(comes in, carrying her coat and bag)*:   Max, have you got your shoes — ah, Norma — don't take your coat off, we're having tea at Auntie Ada's.

NORMA: Hello, Mum.

MIRIAM: Hello, my darling, how was the trip, how's Martin, don't tell me now, you'll have to tell it all again for Auntie Ada.

NORMA *(inspects MIRIAM's blouse)*:   Lovely. The colour suits you.

MIRIAM: It's very nice. You even sent the right size. *(She is wearing the blouse outside the skirt)*.

MAX: Tuck it in.

MIRIAM: It fits, doesn't it?

MAX: Like a dog's dinner. Tuck it in your skirt.

MIRIAM: I like it like this.

MAX: You'll tuck it in your skirt.

MIRIAM: They wear them like this nowadays.

NORMA: That's why it's cut like that, straight at the bottom.

MIRIAM: I always like St Michael.

MAX: St Michael. Whoever heard of a Yiddische saint. You don't see me going out with St Michael hanging out.

NORMA: We're only going to Auntie Ada's.

MAX: Don't argue. *(To MIRIAM.)* You wear it how I say or you can go by yourself.

NORMA: She's wearing it, not you.

MAX: She'll tuck it in.

NORMA: New trousers, Max?

MAX: You like them? Made them myself? Two pounds a yard in the Lane. She made the buttonholes.

NORMA: You going to wear your shirt outside, then?

MAX: What do you think, I'm daft?

NORMA: You'll tuck it in?

MAX: Sure I'll tuck it in.

NORMA: You should wear it outside.

MAX: Do me a favour.

NORMA: You should.

MAX: Don't tell me how I should wear this and how I should wear that.

NORMA: So don't you go telling —

MIRIAM: Norma, we got some news to tell you. You remember Gerry Simons —

MAX: Don't you interfere.

MIRIAM: He's mad, your father. I'll tell you in the car. Come on.

MAX: You shut all the windows?

MIRIAM: Yes.

MAX: You got the pension book?

MIRIAM: Yes.

MAX: The cheque book?

NORMA
MIRIAM *(together)*: The post-office book, the back-door key . . .

MIRIAM: Yes.

MAX: So why are we waiting?

MIRIAM: I must say goodbye to the tomato plants.

MAX: She's mad, your mother. Gerry Simons, he's got news about your mother's sister, the one we thought got eaten up in the war.

NORMA: Who's Gerry Simons?

MIRIAM: I'll tell her, it's my news.

MAX: She'll tell you, it's her news.

As they leave the room, there is a ring at the door. MIRIAM *comes back in, half-supporting* JOSH, *whose hands have blood on them. He is clutching a carrier bag.* JOSH *is a young orthodox Jew, unbearded, with long side-curls, a skullcap, white shirt, black trousers and a black three-quarter length overcoat.*

JOSH: Shma . . . shma, shma Yisroel . . . shma . . . who is this, is this Buba?

MIRIAM: Josh, Joshua, this is Mrs Selby, Josh, what's happened to you?

JOSH: Mrs Selby?

NORMA *(to MAX)*: Who on earth is this?

MAX: It's Joshua, Joshua Friedman.

MIRIAM: Josh, let me have a look at your head — oh, the poor boy, what happened to you?

MAX: Mr and Mrs Friedman's son, he went to Israel, they used to live in Palatine Road —

MIRIAM: Max, we don't want a bibliography, we want a flannel.

JOSH: Don't let them in, you won't let them in?

MIRIAM: Norma, go and make some tea.

MAX *brings a J-cloth from the kitchen,* NORMA *goes out.*

JOSH: Please? You won't let them in?

MIRIAM: Who? Let who? Of course I won't let no-one in.

MAX: Anyone, you won't let anyone in.

MIRIAM: Come on, Josh, pick your head up so I can see properly.

MAX: Where have you been, Josh? Who done this?

NORMA *comes back with a bowl of water.*

MIRIAM: Never mind who done it.

NORMA *(to MAX)*: Perhaps we should call the police.

JOSH: The police — you mustn't get the police, some of them speak Arabic, you don't know who they are. *(He tries to get up to run away, but MIRIAM and MAX soothe him, and he sits down again.)*

MIRIAM: What, police, Josh, tell us where you been.

JOSH: They don't know I'm here. Can I stay here?

MAX: What happened? Tell us.

JOSH: There was a fight, and I ran away, and there was some music, a lot of lights . . .

MIRIAM: Where? Which street?

JOSH: Then I didn't feel so good, I wanted to go home and I went in the street and they hit me, a bottle, I think. I don't want to go home now.

MIRIAM: You don't have to go home, Josh.

NORMA: Do you know who attacked you?

JOSH doesn't seem to hear her.

MIRIAM: Norma, get the tea. *(NORMA goes.)*

MAX: Try to think of a name, a street, something.

JOSH: By the market, some arms —

MAX: The Kings Arms? You went in a pub?

JOSH: It was very bright, and something bitter, not like Pesach wine.

NORMA brings tea. MIRIAM gives some to JOSH, who still clutches his carrier bag.

MAX: Maybe he'll need stitches.

MIRIAM: It's alright. It's just a cut.

JOSH: I want to go to sleep.

The phone rings. NORMA answers it.

NORMA: 3104. Hello. Oh, Auntie Ada, yes, this is Norma.

MAX: Ada. Miriam, she'll have apoplexy.

NORMA: It's my fault, Auntie. I was late — yes, yes, I drove safely —

MIRIAM *(to JOSH)*: Give me your bag, Josh.

JOSH: No, no.

NORMA: We'll be over in a few minutes.

MIRIAM: Tell her I'm not feeling too good.

NORMA: Mum isn't feeling too good — no, nothing serious, just a headache.

JOSH: I didn't tell them Buba and Zaida are away.

MIRIAM: You come and have a little lie down, Josh.

JOSH: There was a man called O'Reilly there —

She takes him off.

NORMA: Yes, I'll come and see you anyway. Yes, a piece of honey cake will be lovely. *(She puts the phone down.)*

MAX: Your Auntie Ada's honey cake would make a bee feel sick.

NORMA: Max, who is Josh?

MIRIAM *(puts her head in)*: You don't tell Ada about Josh, right? She'll be round mixing her nose in. *(She goes.)*

MAX: Joshua Friedman is Mr and Mrs Friedman's grandson. You remember Morris Friedman, he married Sheila Black, they went to Israel in 1949. Josh was born there.

NORMA: What's he doing here?

MAX: Look, you know the Friedmans are a meshuganeh family. So Morris was always a religious fanatic, so he went running when Israel got independent. Now Israel isn't religious enough for him, so he sends Josh back here to study. He has to come back to England to learn how to be a Jew. Look, don't ask me.

NORMA: Sounds a bit upside down to me.

MAX: It's all upside down. So what. Jews left the ghettoes in Europe to live a free life in Israel, and now they got a ghetto in Jerusalem for Jews who are so religious they don't even recognise Israel. Them and the Arabs. Mad.

NORMA: And Josh?

MAX: Josh is here to study, see a bit of life.

NORMA: Well, he looks like he's done that today. Max, don't you think we should call the police, find out who attacked him?

MIRIAM *(coming in, carrying JOSH's carrier bag)*: He doesn't make no sense to us, you think he'll make sense to a silly policeman?

She opens the carrier, and takes out a camouflage combat jacket, a black beret, a pair of dark glasses and a small gun.

MIRIAM: Is this a gun?

MAX: No, it's a potato peeler.

NORMA: It can't be a real gun.

MAX: How would you know? *(He takes the gun.)*

MIRIAM *(has found a piece of paper)*: 'Two pounds of cooking apples, white sugar, a box of birthday candles.'

MAX: It's a real gun. Who is this O'Ridley?

MIRIAM: O'Reilly. You're thinking of Ridley Road, the market. Poor boy, he doesn't know if he's in Timbuctoo.

MAX: What's the difference? He's getting mixed up with mad Irishmen.

NORMA: Max, no Irishman goes round London carrying a real gun.

MAX: So where did he get this? Where are his books?

NORMA: I don't know. Maybe the Special Branch planted it on someone in the pub.

MAX: How can you plant a gun? Miriam, you're the gardener, how can you plant a gun?

NORMA: Perhaps it belongs to a theatre group doing a play about Northern Ireland.

MIRIAM: With a shopping list?

NORMA: Even theatre groups have to eat.

The phone rings.

Tell Ada I've gone.

MIRIAM *(answers phone)*: Hello? Ada? No, no, just a silly headache — no, Max loves your honey cake. Norma? She left ten minutes ago.

JOSH *(off)*: Mrs Selby.

MIRIAM: Thank you, Ada, if I want to lie down in a dark room, I don't need you to — yes, bye-bye.

She goes off.

NORMA: I nearly forgot. Martin got this for you. *(A phial of coloured sand.)* From the Isle of Wight. He went with his school.

MAX: Goyische sand.

NORMA: Sand is sand.

MIRIAM *(coming back in)*: Josh is lying down in our bedroom. Norma, don't say nothing to Ada about Gerry Simons.

NORMA: Mum, I don't know anything to tell.

MAX: I'll tell you, quick.

MIRIAM: She'll be late.

MAX: Gerry Simons may have some news about Leah, your mother's sister and Ada's sister, but your mother doesn't want Ada to know in case it's a false alarm and Ada will have a heart attack.

NORMA: Ada's one of the healthiest old bags I know.

MAX: Don't show no disrespect for the old cow.

NORMA: I'll see you later.

She goes. MAX *picks up the gun.*

MIRIAM: You put that down.

MAX: It's not real. Norma said so.

MIRIAM: I don't like no guns. *(She stuffs all the things back in the carrier.)*

MAX: Martin got us some sand.

MIRIAM: Ah, how sweet.

MAX: Our Norma married a man who doesn't mind being a nursemaid.

MIRIAM: He's the boy's father, why shouldn't he look after him for a few days? Men are different these days.

MAX: You're telling me. He'll circumcise his son, but he won't give him a Yiddische upbringing.

MIRIAM: Listen, Martin didn't want a bar-mitzvah. So what?

MAX: I says to him, Martin, where did you come in the class? He says, we don't have that. What kind of school is it when you don't come nowhere in class?

MIRIAM: I'm worried the tomatoes aren't growing so well this year.

MAX: So then I says, Martin, when are you going to start studying for your bar-mitzvah? Oh, he says, I'm not having a bar-mitzvah, I'm an atheist. Ten years old, he's an atheist.

MIRIAM: He's bright, that boy.

MAX: Sure he's bright. I told her. I said, he can do it standing on his head. Yes, says Norma, he could do it hanging from the chandeliers, but he doesn't want a bar-mitzvah.

MIRIAM: Norma hasn't got no chandeliers.

MAX: If you can convince Norma to make him a bar-mitzvah, your tomatoes will grow Jaffa oranges on them. A Jewish boy, he doesn't learn Hebrew, how's he going to know what he is? I produce a daughter, an intellectual, she marries a man who don't understand no Yiddish. That's no Jew.

MIRIAM: He's been intimidated.

MAX: Assimilated.

MIRIAM: He's English.

MAX: I'm English. But I know who I am. Martin should know what it is to have Yiddishkeit. If he doesn't know what it is, how can he know he doesn't want it?

MIRIAM: In a month, maybe, I'll transplant the tomatoes.

MAX: You don't care about your grandson.

MIRIAM: I care. He should be healthy and happy. That's all. Shall I make supper?

MAX: Why not.

MIRIAM *removes the radio from the table; as she does so,* MAX *looks at the newspaper* NORMA *has left.*

The Royal babies have it cut off. That doesn't make them Jewish, does it? Look at this. The whole world's mad. 'Airplane from Los Angeles hi-jacked.' Mad. All of them.

MIRIAM: Los Angeles? *(She rushes to the sideboard, looking for something.)* What else does it say? Max, where did you put the letter?

MAX: Letter? What letter?

MIRIAM: The letter from Gerry Simons. *(She starts dialling.)*

MAX: Now who are you phoning?

MIRIAM: Hello. Excuse me. Is this the airport? Yes. I want to find out about the hi-jack — yes — well, I'm not certain, I'll give you his name. Simons. S-I-M-O-N-S. Simons. *(To* MAX.*)* In the letter. It's this week he's coming, right?

MAX: I can't remember. I'm not his watchdog.

MIRIAM *(to phone)*: Yes. yes. That's right. Thank you very much. Yes. Goodbye.

MAX: He's on it?

MIRIAM: Unless it's another man with the same name?

MAX: No. Forty years, the man doesn't change. Gerry Simons always has to be the centre of attention.

MIRIAM: You think he arranged the hi-jack?

MAX: Anything to get his name in the papers.

MIRIAM: Oh, do me a favour. Gerry Simons wouldn't plan a hi-jack.

MAX: No. He's too much of a schmuck.

MIRIAM: So don't talk daft. Why didn't he send us a telegram he's coming.

MAX: The only way Gerry Simons would send a telegram is to deliver it himself, he's so mean.

MIRIAM: Well, we'll have to wait. Be calm. I waited thirty years to hear about my sister, I'll wait a little bit longer.

MAX: Where did they say it's landing?

MIRIAM: Stansted.

MAX: Stansted in England?

MIRIAM: No, Stansted in China.

MAX: They don't stop, the anti-semites.

MIRIAM: What?

MAX: Money, they wanted. More Palestinians. More money, because any excuse to attack Israel.

MIRIAM: What are you talking about? It's not a Palestinian.

MAX: You got a hot line to him? You know who he is?

MIRIAM: Of course not.

MAX: So you listen to me. It's another Palestinian. He should sweat.

MIRIAM: Like everyone else on the plane?

MAX: So you think we should give in?

MIRIAM: We?

MAX: Us Britishers.

MIRIAM: Look, first, we don't know what they want. Second, of course we should give in. There are women and children on that plane.

MAX: And Gerry Simons.

MIRIAM: Perhaps this is a warning. You shouldn't try and bring back sisters from the dead.

MAX: Look, they do it properly, and they can squeeze the guerrillas out. I tell you, that schlock Simons will get himself on Nationwide.

MIRIAM: They'll have to give in. Money's not as important as life.

MAX: Give him the money, Barney. Listen, you give in to one you give in to all. They got to do like the Israelis at Entebbe, the Germans at Mogadishu. Hold out.

MIRIAM: Mogadishu, they killed the pilot. He was married.

MAX: You been talking to your socialistic daughter again. You and she want they should drive us all into the sea.

MIRIAM: Nobody's driving us into the sea. Look at all the Jews settled happily in Brighton. Ach, I don't want to talk politics.

MAX: Why should they hi-jack? For money. For guns. To attack somebody. Why should he come to England to get money? It's to get his own back for Suez, and for the British Mandate in Palestine — instead, he should go for peace, like Sadat —

MIRIAM: 'When they begin the Begin . . .'

MAX: You should take politics seriously.

MIRIAM: I take my family seriously. And I don't cross all my eggs in one basket before I come to them.

MAX: My wife the scholar.

MIRIAM: So we're going to starve? Bring the radio, we'll have supper in the kitchen.

They exit.

Scene Two

It is night. JOSH *is lying on the couch, restless. He wakes, unsure about where he is. Then he searches for the carrier bag, finds it and takes out the camouflage jacket and puts it on. He goes back to sleep.*

Scene Three

NORMA *and* MAX *are having breakfast.* JOSH *is eating with them, still wearing the camouflage jacket.* MIRIAM *joins them.*

MIRIAM: So you don't remember how you got here?

JOSH: I can't remember anything after the bottle hit me.

NORMA: Why didn't you go home, to your grandparents?

JOSH: I don't know.

MAX: And the hall you were in — you remember the name?

JOSH: Outside was a board. It said 'The truth about the six million'. I was just interested.

NORMA: Oh, my God.

JOSH: I didn't want to go home yet. It's dark when I get back from classes.

MIRIAM: You're a silly boy to get lonely. I told your grandparents you should visit us any time you get lonely, or maybe you want a chat.

NORMA: When are they coming home?

JOSH: What day is it?

NORMA: Thursday.

MAX: So what happened in the meeting?

JOSH: Well, there was a man talking about immigrants. He said all immigrants must go back to their own country. He said all Indians must go back to India. And then another man said if all the Jews went to Uganda in the first place, like Theodore Herzl said, we wouldn't have any problems in the world.

NORMA: Herzl didn't know about Amin, did he?

JOSH: I asked a question.

MAX: What question? You sugared my tea, Miriam?

MIRIAM: Yes.

JOSH: I said, who are the immigrants, please?

NORMA: Have you ever been to a political meeting before, Josh?

JOSH: So he said the niggers and anyone else who didn't belong. So I said I am a Jew, and where do I belong, and then it was all shouting and someone said 'That's a Jew living off stolen property', and then there was hitting and I hit and there was police and then I ran —

MAX: Just a minute, just a minute, you hit?

JOSH: I hit one. With a chair.

MIRIAM: Didn't the police help you?

MAX: Sssh. You hit one?

JOSH: He tried to take my books. I hit him with a chair. He fell down.

MAX: Good boy, you done good.

JOSH: No, it's bad to fight, it's a sin. I won't serve in the Israeli army when they call me. It's a sin.

NORMA: It depends who you're fighting for.

MAX: A Jew is attacked, a Jew fights. You see, Josh, a Jew learns quickly.

JOSH: No. I don't think so. Anyway, I kept my books. *(He picks up the carrier.)* No-one is going to take my Talmud.

The phone rings. MIRIAM *answers it.*

MIRIAM: Hello, this is Mrs Selby speaking. Oh, Ada. Yes, good morning, yes, much better, thank you. Look, I can't have a long conversazione because I'm expecting an important telephone communication. You what? Sit down? Alright. *(She listens.)* Ada, you're telling me? Ada, I've known for three weeks he was coming — so you're telling me to keep calm. Well, I didn't want to worry you with no false alarm — you know how nervous you are — well, anyway, we'll just have to wait. Yes, thank you, Ada. Goodbye. *(To* NORMA.*)* So why didn't you tell me she got a letter from Gerry Simons as well, and she knows I know?

NORMA: She was waiting for you to tell her. She made me promise not to tell you.

MAX: Both you two sisters are mad.

JOSH: I have to go now.

MIRIAM: Go?

JOSH: To classes.

MIRIAM: What about your head?

JOSH: I'm fine now, Mrs Selby.

MIRIAM: And what about after classes? With no key.

JOSH: Oh.

MIRIAM: So I have a suggestion. Go and study upstairs, stay a bit.

NORMA: We could have a theological debate about the marine life in the Red Sea.

MAX: Don't be silly, Norma.

JOSH: Thank you, Mrs Selby.

NORMA *(indicating jacket)*: You won't need this upstairs, you know.

JOSH: It's mine. It was in my bag. I could go to war in this and no-one would recognise me.

NORMA: But Jews don't fight, Josh.

MAX: Leave him alone. Go on.

JOSH *goes.*

MIRIAM: Did you notice? He ate breakfast.

NORMA: So?

MIRIAM: You know how frum Mr and Mrs Friedman are. They don't even drink a cup of tea when they come.

NORMA: Maybe Josh is having a rest from religion.

MAX: He's a good kid.

MIRIAM: You should try your jacket on, Norma. Maybe it'll be ready before you go tomorrow. Then I can do the button-holes tonight.

NORMA: Alright.

MAX *puts the half-made jacket on* NORMA, *then takes the yardstick, box of pins, tailor's chalk, puts the tape measure round his neck.* MAX *adjusts the front of the jacket to mark where the button-holes should come, arranging the front so that the left side overlaps the right side.*

Hey, not that way.

MAX: What do you mean, not that way?

NORMA: This way. *(She reverses the jacket, so that the right side overlaps the left.)*

MAX: But that's the woman's way.

NORMA: That's right.

MAX: That's a gents' jacket, you know.

NORMA: You're making it for me. I'm not a gent.

MAX: You're telling me. You're no lady neither. You're lucky I make anything for you.

NORMA: I know, chuch. You're a wonderful tailor.

MAX: Pattern cutter.

MAX *marks the first button-hole with chalk and a pin. He marks the other two, measuring two inches between them with the yardstick, from the floor.*

NORMA: Sorry. Pattern cutter.

MAX: My daughter, the clever teacher, she doesn't know the difference between a tailor and a pattern-cutter.

When he has finished the button-holes he gets down on his knees to mark the length of the hem evenly, again using the yardstick, and marking the hem round with pieces of chalk, when NORMA *has indicated how long she wants it. At intervals he says 'Turn', so that* NORMA *moves round for him to mark the length of the entire hem. When he's finished, he takes the jacket and begins basting the hem.*

NORMA: So what is the difference?

MAX: A pattern cutter cuts patterns, he can even make patterns, he can even sometimes do his own designs. A tailor macht.

NORMA: He?

MAX: Sure, he. A pattern-cutter was a he. I'm talking fifty years ago, not in women's lib time. I didn't go three years to night-school, a cheese sandwich, a cup of milk, classes till nine and home by ten, so you should call me a tailor. These — *(He brandishes the scissors.)* — this is what I am. Turn.

MIRIAM *(off)*:   Then he wonders why he nearly got an ulcer.

MAX: You keep quiet and cook.

MIRIAM: Wash. I'm washing up.

MAX: So wash. Anyway, I learned to be a tailor before I was a pattern-cutter. I can do it all. Not like youngsters today.

NORMA: Young people today just don't know they're born, eh?

MAX: Like some people I wouldn't care to mention. How is your husband?

NORMA: He's got a name, you know.

MAX: Sure he's got a name. It's just a religion he hasn't got.

NORMA: Don't start, eh?

MAX: It's not right.

NORMA: It's not on.

MAX: Just because you want your son to be a socialist doesn't mean he can't know what it is to be a Jew.

NORMA: Martin knows he's Jewish. He knows we're Jewish. And he knows you and Mum observe Pesach and Yom Kippur and not much else.

MAX: Don't insult your mother.

NORMA: You know what I mean. He doesn't want a bar-mitzvah.

MAX: You don't want a bar-mitzvah.

NORMA: I can live without a bar-mitzvah.

MAX: And when all his little school pals start calling him a Yid, what then?

NORMA: He beats them up.

MAX: What?

NORMA: When they call him a Yid.

MAX: They call him a Yid?

NORMA: Martin being called a Yid by some kid in his football team, and Josh getting beaten up at some fascist meeting are not entirely unconnected.

MAX: Say that again in English.

NORMA: You know what I mean.

MAX: So you prove my point.

NORMA: You don't have to have a bar-mitzvah to thump racist kids.

MAX: Karl Marx, Rosa Luxembourg, Leon Trotsky, Leon Blum —

NORMA: Were all Jewish. I know.

MAX: And look at the early Zionists — so many of them —

NORMA: — thought they were socialists. I know.

MAX: They were socialists.

NORMA: They were then. They wouldn't be now. Today you can't be a socialist and be religious.

MAX: And what about the Catholics in South America?

NORMA: Oh — you still read the newspapers. Anyway, I'm talking about here, in Europe.

MAX: You don't come Chanukah, you don't come Pesach —

NORMA: I don't go to shool, I don't fast. You do. Fine. I'm not you.

MIRIAM (*off*): Women's lib.

MAX: You keep quiet. I'll burn your bra, you're not careful.

MIRIAM (*off*): They don't burn bras in England, only in America they burn bras. Norma told me.

MAX: And these hi-jackers — that's your idea of socialism, I suppose?

NORMA: Hi-jacking planes isn't socialism.

MAX: I'll tell you about socialism.

MIRIAM (*off*): She wants to go out, buy some things.

MAX: You visit your father once in a blue moon, you can listen to a little bit of history for a change. Fifty years ago, in 1927, I worked by Finkelstein, Max Finkelstein, he changed his name to Fine before the war, his father knew Theodore Herzl, the founder of Zionism, so Maxie had a workshop off Commercial Road, Lilac Alley, it's knocked down now. So I worked there, and Gerry, Gerald Simons, he was after the Finkelstein's eldest daughter, and the Finkelstein boys worked there, a family firm, I was the only stranger worked there. After the war, Fine went into dresses, retail dresses.

NORMA: And?

MAX: And nothing. Simons lost me my job.

NORMA: How?

MAX: My stomach was really bad that time, I couldn't eat. I couldn't keep anything down, so I went to the hospital for tests. And one day she comes to visit me and she says, hello, Max, they've sent your scissors home.

NORMA: Your scissors?

MAX: Every tailor had his own tools — ah, you didn't know that, did you? Before electricity a tailor had to buy his own gas mantels. Scissors, you had your own scissors, cottons, you had to buy your own cottons as well. So they sent my scissors back. So finished.

NORMA: You mean you got the sack?

MAX: Clever. Gerald was jealous, I worked faster, I was a much better worker than him, so he told them, 'Look, Max Selby is ill, what are you holding his job for, send him his scissors back, I'll do the job for you for less money.'

NORMA: How do you know he said that?

MAX: Because I came home, I find out Gerald is working there for a pound less a week.

NORMA: So what did you do?

MAX: What could I do? I got better. I got another job.

NORMA: And the union?

MAX: What could they do? A small family firm. They couldn't do nothing. That's socialism for you. It's not as though he stayed in the trade, even. He went to America, set himself up in jewellery.

NORMA: And now he's bringing you tidings of joy.

MAX: I tell you, I wouldn't have him in the house if it wasn't for your mother.

NORMA: What will you say to him?

MAX: When did you know me not polite? 'How's business, Gerry Simons? How's the family?' You should realise you got a mensch for a father. A human being. Now.

He tries the jacket on NORMA *to check for length.* MIRIAM *comes in.*

MIRIAM: Gerry Simons is just as much a mensch as Max Selby. He did what he had to do. Now he brings me news from a ghost.

NORMA: You seem very calm about it.

MIRIAM: I finished with messy feelings on May twenty-third, 1946.

MAX: See, your mother has a sense of history.

He takes the jacket and the second sleeve and goes off. We hear the sound of a sewing machine.

MIRIAM: One year I spent, after the war, trying to trace the family. The Jewish Agency, the Red Cross, nothing. You know, my great-grandparents had a farm in Russia. They were driven off that. My father ended up selling firewood. Then the whole family went up in smoke in the war. Except for Ada. So on May 23rd 1946 I had a little word with God and I said, thank you, God, you left me one sister, that's very generous, now you can just keep the hell — excuse me — out of my kitchen. I broke a whole set of dishes. Fleischedike ones. We didn't keep a kosher kitchen since then. His parents were dead — *(Indicating* MAX *off.)* — so who cared?

MAX *(off)*: Tell her how Ada got out.

MIRIAM: Months and months, I went to Bloomsbury House, week in, week out — that was the place that got people over. A lot of Jews were applying to get relatives out, in 1939 already.

MAX *(off)*: Before the war.

MIRIAM: Anyway, you know there was heavy unemployment here, they wanted you should promise you had where for them to live, and that they had enough money so they didn't work.

MAX *(off)*: In the end I went to the Home Office —

MIRIAM: In the end Daddy went to the Home Office, to arrange —

MAX *(off)*: . . . to arrange it.

MIRIAM: Ada had a little sweet shop in Berlin, the Nazis they walked in one day and said 'Juden Raus', so she said 'Do you mind if I take my apron off?' Anyway, in the war all the English girls were going into the factories, so there was a shortage of domestic servants, so Ada went as a general domestic to a Lord and Lady Muck somewhere. This Lady, she had to do her own cooking and she was so mean —

MAX *(off)*: She was so mean —

MIRIAM: She was so mean she used to count the rice for the rice pudding.

MAX: She was so mean she used to discount the rice for the —

MIRIAM: I just said that. Anyway, you know the rest. Auntie Ada is Auntie Ada.

MAX comes in with the jacket, the second sleeve in. He gives it to MIRIAM.

MAX: You do three buttonholes, you sew three buttons on each sleeve — here, and you fell in the hem.

MIRIAM: Don't teach your grandmother to suck cotton. I've finished more jackets than I changed nappies.

MAX: Don't embarrass her.

MIRIAM: So you can see why I'm calm. Ada's the meshuganeh, the least thing makes her jumpy.

The phone rings. MIRIAM *drops the jacket and rushes to the phone.*

Hello? Hello? Ah, it's you, Ada. We was just talking about you. Oh, just old times, a little family history. Oh. That's very nice of you. Yes. Now just you calm down, it'll be alright.

She puts the phone down.

I tell you a funny thing, Norma. When Gerry wrote to us first saying he had news of my sister, you know what was funny? I forgot her name. Leah. She's called Leah. After thirty years, just her name was like a gift.

JOSH appears in the doorway wearing the beret and dark glasses, the jacket done up, carrying the gun awkwardly.

MIRIAM: Josh. You do look — nice.

JOSH: How do you know my name?

MIRIAM: You should put that thing down, Josh. *(Gesturing to gun.)*

JOSH: A Jew is attacked, a Jew fights. *(To* MAX.*)* That's what you said? That's what Zaida says. Dad says a Jew must not fight, that's why he sent me here, underground, here I can be a Jew with no desert and no tanks.

MAX: Perhaps he needs a doctor?

MIRIAM: He's just a little confused.

JOSH: I'm not confused.

JOSH: This is London 1978, Josh, not Palestine 1917.

JOSH: First we have to go underground, and then we fight for the land of our ancestors, we take it away from the Philistines.

MIRIAM: Come on, Josh, Mr and Mrs Selby, this is our daughter, Norma, remember, you met her this morning?

JOSH: We have no pogroms, we have no ghettoes. We are our own soldiers. The goyim can kill each other. Not the Jews any more.

NORMA: Why don't you go back to Israel and fight?

JOSH: This is my country. I will fight to sweep my enemies from my country.

MAX: Josh, this is Stoke Newington, there's no enemies here.

NORMA: Apart from the fascists who beat him up, of course, and apart from some of his best Yiddische friends, there's not a single enemy in sight.

JOSH *(shouts)*: Every people must be free of persecution. *(He rummages in the bag.)* I must get bullets, grenades.

MIRIAM: Norma, don't annoy him. I'll make a cup of tea. *(She goes out.)*

NORMA: Josh, tell us, who are your enemies.

JOSH *(not looking at her)*: The people who want to drive us into the sea. First in Europe, all over Europe, I read it in the books, then the Nazis, then the people who wouldn't give us somewhere to run from the Nazis, and now it's the Arabs, it's different faces, it's the same thing.

MAX: It's true. The first and second Aliyah to Israel, Palestine as it was, that was the first chance the Jews had to live in peace, know they had a land. They had to take it back.

NORMA: So the Jews exchanged their exile for a home, and to do that, they had to send other people into exile. Is that an eye for an eye and a tooth for a tooth? Is that your land, Josh?

MAX: Norma, Israel is Israel.

JOSH: Just leave us in peace.

NORMA *(grabs JOSH)*: Josh, look at me. Why won't you look me in the eyes? Why are you embarrassed to look at a woman? Even me. I'm old enough to be your mother, nearly. What are you frightened of?

JOSH *(rocking back and forth, almost intoning)*: A daughter of Zion does not show her arms, a daughter of Zion wears her sheitl to cover her hair when she marries, you're traif and dirty, you know nothing about God. I thank God I was not born a woman.

NORMA: So do I, Josh, because no woman could live with the shame that you feel. If you won't look at me, think about the people who did this — *(Indicating his head.)* — about why your parents emigrated to Israel and hate it because Israel is not religious enough for them, ask yourself why it isn't flowing with milk and honey, ask yourself whether the Jews are the only semitic people entitled to a home, a Jew is supposed to ask questions, ask yourself some bloody questions.

JOSH: No more Warsaw ghettoes —

NORMA: No more refugees.

MAX: Norma, my Norma, I don't understand you. You don't say Palestine is for the Palestinians, you don't say Israel is for Jews. How could I produce such a liberal?

NORMA: History has happened. Israel is there. But its future has to be for both, not excluding Jews or Arabs.

MAX: That's your socialism.

NORMA: That's my socialism. And if Josh comes to his senses, he can do something about it. God help him.

JOSH: Women do not talk to God. *(He gets under the table.)*

MAX: Not that I want the old days back, but in the old days, when you could see who was persecuting you, then you knew who you were.

NORMA: Bullshit.

MIRIAM *(comes in with tea)*: What's Josh doing under the table?

NORMA: Having a little think about the state of the world.

MAX: Norma was a little pushy.

MIRIAM: He's only a kid.

NORMA: Exactly. He's got time to learn.

MIRIAM: Josh, you like a nice cup of tea? Norma didn't mean it.

NORMA: Oh yes she did.

MIRIAM: The news. *(She switches the radio on.)*

MAX: You want Israel should be a godless state?

NORMA: I think religion is out of date.

MIRIAM: Sssh.

ANNOUNCER: . . . no casualties among the passengers. The hi-jackers, both wounded, have been taken away by the police.

MIRIAM: Thank God.

MAX: Stormed, like the Israelis at Entebbe.

NORMA: And the Germans at Mogadishu.

MIRIAM: Oh, stop it. People die in these things, and to you it's just a game. Norma, tidy up. Max, you ring Ada — no, I'll ring to tell her.

NORMA: I can see I'm not going anywhere today.

JOSH: Don't you touch my Talmud.

Scene Four

The table is laid with a salad and plates; NORMA's jacket is back on the stand. JOSH sits on the floor in a corner, with his bag, his knees drawn up. MAX and MIRIAM are sitting at the table.

MAX: Would you like the radio? The Archers is on.

MIRIAM *shakes her head.*

MAX: A cup of tea?

MIRIAM *shakes her head.*

I'm hungry. *(He reaches a hand to the salad.* MIRIAM *slaps him.)*

MIRIAM: Wait.

MAX: Can I sneak a cake when Norma gets back?

MIRIAM: We could have one piece of cucumber each.

MAX *elaborately takes two pieces, gives one to* MIRIAM, *then gestures towards* JOSH.

MAX: Joshua? *(No reply.)* Who are you sitting shiva for? Nobody's died.

MIRIAM: Leave him. He just wants to be alone.

MAX: We'll have to do something about him.

MIRIAM: He's alright. Aren't you, Josh? *(No reply.)* See. He just wants to be alone.

MAX: Mr Greta Garbo.

Pause.

Maybe Gerry Simons has decided he doesn't like London, it's too dangerous . . . maybe . . .

The doorbell rings. MIRIAM *jumps.*

MIRIAM: Now you be polite, Max. Go on.

MAX *goes to open the front door. Sounds of greeting, then he and* GERRY *enter.* GERRY *is wearing loud American clothes, unshaven.*

MAX: So you're Gerry Simons.

GERRY: Who did you think I was, President of the United States?

MIRIAM: Mr Simons, how nice to see you — may I take your coat?

GERRY: How are you, Mrs Selby? It's been a long time.

MIRIAM: Miriam, please, Mr Simons.

GERRY: Miriam. Of course. And I'm still Gerry to my old friends.

MIRIAM: Thank God you got here. Max, take Gerry's coat.

GERRY: I'm afraid — a whole day on the plane — no chance to wash. *(He indicates the coat,* MAX *holds it gingerly, as if it might smell.)* Same old Max, eh?

MAX: Not so much of the old.

He and GERRY *spontaneously hug, and then both pretend it didn't happen.* MAX *goes to hang the coat up.*

MIRIAM: Well, that's nice. You'd like to come and have a wash?

GERRY: I'll take a shower later, if that's convenient.

MIRIAM: A bath.

GERRY: Ah, that's right, you don't have showers over here.

MAX: We don't have dollars neither.

MIRIAM: Sit down. I made a nice salad. You want some tea?

MAX: Don't you want to hear about your sister?

MIRIAM: I can wait three more minutes. *(She bustles off. The men sit at the table.)*

MAX: So. You're a big shot in the land of opportunity?

GERRY: Well, I'd say I was a modest success.

MAX: You got a swimming pool?

GERRY: I got two.

MAX: Disgusting.

GERRY: Listen, I got a three-room little apartment in a big apartment block. The block has a swimming pool. One.

MAX: Still a liar, ha?

GERRY: You still got no sense of humour, ha?

MIRIAM *enters with tea.*

MIRIAM: My sister Ada is coming over, she said she heard from you. Milk, lemon?

GERRY: Without nothing, thank you all the same.

MAX: His English hasn't got no better.

NORMA *enters with a box of cakes.* GERRY *rises.*

MIRIAM: Ah, Norma, this is my daughter Norma. Norma, Gerry Simons. You never seen her, eh?

GERRY: I'm very delighted to meet you, I'm sure.

NORMA: Nice to see you, Mr Simons.

MIRIAM: She must be about the same age as your Harold. Did he marry?

GERRY: Oh yes. He married a beautiful girl.

MAX: You got nachas?

GERRY: Nachas? Mustn't grumble. I got two grandsons. Miriam, I got a personal letter for you. Here.

MIRIAM *(takes letter, reads in silence)*: Ah.

MAX *(unable to restrain his curiosity)*: Nu?

MIRIAM: It's in Polish. You want I should translate?

MAX: I come to England when I'm six months old, she wants I should remember Polish.

MIRIAM *(translating)*: 'My dear one, Miriam, how good it is to find where you are.'

MAX *(to GERRY)*: Did you have a good flight?

MIRIAM: 'I send you photographs of our family, which — whom, of course, you have never seen. My oldest daughter works here in Leningrad as an interpreter, and this is how she met the son of your good friend Mr Simons.'

MAX *(to GERRY)*: We heard you had a spot of trouble.

NORMA: Sssh.

MAX: *Blonde* children?

GERRY: My son informed me that Leah is married to a Communist.

MAX: A Communist? That's all we need, eh, Miri?

NORMA: But you can be a Communist and a Jew, Max. You told me.

MIRIAM: Is she happy? Ah, of course, how should you know. Harold, what did he say?

GERRY: He only met her for a short time. They have a small apartment. She's a member of the Communist Party as well.

NORMA: See? You were right. Clever Daddy.

MIRIAM: Good. Now tell about you.

GERRY: Well, when I left London, I went first to New York to start my little business there —

MIRIAM: No, no, the plane. The hi-jack. We heard all about it on the radio. Thank God it worked out alright, nobody killed.

GERRY: Is that what they said?

NORMA: They said the hi-jackers were wounded.

GERRY: Goddam it. They killed one of them. They told us later, when we came off the plane.

MIRIAM: Oh.

MAX: Palestinian guerrillas. They should have killed them both.

GERRY: Palestinian guerrillas? Who are you talking about?

MAX: Baader Meinhof then. Japanese madmen.

GERRY: No, no, nothing like that. Brothers, they were two brothers from India.

MAX: From India?

GERRY: Yes. Well, they live here so they're not Indians, they're British. Their sister is locked up in some jail here, the British authorities are going to send her back to India. She is pregnant. They told us the authorities don't believe she is their sister. You get it?

MAX: No.

NORMA: Why were they in Los Angeles?

GERRY: Well, they figured, where would they get a lot of publicity? Big America. So they borrow the money to fly to Los Angeles. Make a big splash. Hey, we nearly did, eh?

MAX: Why didn't they go to New York? That's America. It's cheaper.

GERRY: Don't ask me. I don't understand foreigners.

NORMA: What did they want the money for?

GERRY: Money? They didn't ask for no money. What's with your communications system here?

NORMA: So they killed one of them.

GERRY: Yeah. It's terrible. He was a nice kid. Except for the gun. They're gonna send the sister back anyway.

MIRIAM: Well, I'm glad it worked out alright.

JOSH *stands, holding the gun.*

NORMA: Mum, it hasn't worked out alright.

MIRIAM: I mean, Gerry's safe. What could I do about it? *(She sees* JOSH.*)* Josh?

MAX: Josh, come and join us.

MIRIAM: Gerry, this is Joshua, a friend of ours, well, the grandson of a friend —

JOSH: Who is this?

MAX: Gerry, Mrs Selby just told —

JOSH: He's from the police.

GERRY: What the hell is going on here?

MIRIAM: He's not well —

NORMA: It's alright, Mr Simons, it's not a real —

GERRY *grabs the gun; taking* JOSH *by surprise.*

MIRIAM: Come on, Josh, come and have a bite with us.

NORMA: For God's sake, Josh, stop being so silly.

JOSH: You stop making fun of me, you traitor.

NORMA: You're a pacifist, Josh, remember?

GERRY: He's a pacifist?

JOSH: You bloody English Jews. None of you take me seriously. You try to turn me into an animal, to take an eye for an eye.

MAX: We take you seriously.

JOSH *(at* GERRY*)*: He takes my gun. *(He fumbles on the sideboard and grabs the scissors.)*

MIRIAM: He was worried for you.

GERRY: Listen, in an army you have a gun, not in a home. You shouldn't play with such things.

JOSH: You're weak, you are. You're all frightened of guns. If you don't fight, you'll be driven into the Red Sea only this time the waters will close over your head. *(He menaces* GERRY *with the scissors.)* You don't deserve your own land. You are not Jews.

MAX: Josh, Gerry is an old friend, a good Zionist. He gave a lot of money to Israel, didn't you, Gerry, tell him. He lives in America now —

JOSH: America? American money? Americans want to buy Israel now. The Communists want to put Palestine into little parcels. You Zionists and Communists are all the same, you don't care what anybody else wants.

JOSH *takes the scissors, and cuts his sidecurls off. Then he takes his skull cap and cuts that in two. He throws the scissors on the floor.*

Now. You tell me. Who is a Jew?

There is a knock at the door. Everyone freezes. The knocking again, louder. MIRIAM *goes.* JOSH *breaks and sits down, again in a stupor.*

MIRIAM *(comes in carrying a carrier bag identical to Josh's, with a book open at the flyleaf)*: It's the police. *(She holds the book out to* JOSH *who takes no notice.)* They want to speak to you, Josh, about the meeting. *(No answer.)* Norma, you go, you speak to them, you know what to say.

AID THY NEIGHBOUR

Aid Thy Neighbour was first performed at the Theatre at New End, London, on October 10th, 1978, with the following cast.

SANDY	Nina Ward
GEORGINA	Patricia Donovan
MARY	Elizabeth Revill
JOSEPH	John Gillet
GERALDINE	Sara Boyes
DAPHNE	Arbel Jones
DOCTOR	Arbel Jones
NURSE	Sara Boyes

Directed by Kate Crutchley
Designed by Mary Moore
Lighting by Nancy Diuguid

ACT ONE

The set is two London living rooms, with the dividing wall, as it were, knocked down. It functions on demand as either the home of SANDY and GEORGINA, or MARY and JOSEPH. At the back of the set are sections which represent the separate kitchens of the two houses. At an upper level of the set are the two couples' bedrooms. Downstage there is a table set for a foursome dinner party.

Scene One

Both halves of the set used simultaneously. Music: Doris Day singing 'Stepping Out with my Baby'.
GEORGINA *and* MARY *enter their halves together;* MARY *in a dress and smart apron empties some peanuts into a dish and takes them to a small coffee-table. She sinks down onto the couch, her eyes shut.*
GEORGINA *takes a book, Adrienne Rich's* 'Of Woman Born', *and sits on a chair to read.*

Sound of a motor-bike stopping. Both women react. Sound of a car stopping, door slamming. Both women react, MARY *jumping up to go to her kitchen and slice a lemon.*

GEORGINA*'s half*

SANDY *(sings off)*: What are little girls made of
                What are little girls made of
                Frogs and snails
                And puppy dogs' tails
                That's what little girls are made of.

    SANDY *enters, wearing a neat dress or skirt and top.*

    'Evening all.

MARY*'s half*

JOSEPH *(sings off)*: What are little boys made of
                What are little boys made of
                Sugar and spice
                And all things nice
                That's what little boys are made of.

    He enters, carrying a flat briefcase and a wrapped bottle of wine and goes to a list pinned up on the wall above his desk. Writes.

    Alan James.

SANDY: Hello, love. *(Comes to kiss GEORGINA.)* Here. *(Gives her a carrier bag.)*

GEORGINA: Great. Just what we need. Had a good day?

SANDY: Oh, so-so.

GEORGINA: Unarmed combat in the staffroom?

SANDY: More like guerrilla warfare in the classroom. How about you?

GEORGINA: Oh, usual.

> MARY *comes forward to put serviettes on the table.* JOSEPH *comes to greet her properly.*

JOSEPH *(hugging her)*: Hello, darling.

MARY: Hello, darling. Mind my hair.

JOSEPH *(sniffs)*: Delicious.

MARY: Had a good day?

JOSEPH: So-so. *(He goes to sit on the couch.)* And you?

MARY: Oh, usual.

SANDY *(sinks onto cushions)*: God, I'm shattered. Where's the opener?

GEORGINA: The what?

SANDY: The bottle.

GEORGINA *(getting up and going to kitchen area)*: We can't open it now.

SANDY: The Labour government's brought in prohibition. I knew it.

GEORGINA: You can't take an open bottle of wine to a dinner party.

SANDY: A dinner party?

GEORGINA *(indicating next door)*: Remember? Meet the neighbours?

SANDY: Oh, God, no.

GEORGINA: Oh, God, yes. You've got time for a bath. *(And she helps heave SANDY up and guide her off through the kitchen. She returns to her chair and her book.)*

JOSEPH: More than busy, actually. Hectic.

MARY: Poor love.

JOSEPH: You know, I've done two synopses of that article and he still isn't satisfied.

MARY: Joe, there isn't time for office gossip now. Go and have a wash.

JOSEPH: It's not gossip, Mary. It's the story about St Cuthbert's. Remember? The ante-natal clinic.

MARY: We're not ante-natal yet, Joe.

JOSEPH: You should always count your chickens.

MARY: I bet you forgot.

JOSEPH: I never forget. *(Shows her a bottle of wine.)*

MARY: That won't be enough.

JOSEPH: Then I'll get some more. Mary, aren't you interested in my work?

MARY *(soothing, dismissive)*: Of course, dear. Now go and change.

SANDY *(pops back in)*: Where's the herbal shampoo?

GEORGINA: Oh, shit.

SANDY: You forgot.

GEORGINA: I forgot.

SANDY: How many books have you read today? *(She slams out.)*

GEORGINA *(calls after her)*: Washed up breakfast, emptied your ashtrays, made the bed, took the washing to the launderette, bought an early evening paper to look at the ads, went shopping. Shall I go on?

No answer.

Developed the photographs. Got the guy's name from Louise and wrote him a letter. *(Pause.)* Len rang.

SANDY *(from off)*: So that's why you forgot my shampoo.

JOSEPH *comes in with a towelling robe on and bare feet.*

JOSEPH: Have you ironed my blue shirt?

MARY: Not with bare feet on the carpet, Joe.

JOSEPH: It's alright, my foot and mouth's nearly cured.

MARY: You know what I mean.

JOSEPH: You've been working the hoover to the bone, I can see.

MARY: I hope you've got a good appetite.

JOSEPH: Massive. Only had a sandwich with Alan and Jenny. She's very bright.

MARY: Jenny?

JOSEPH: Novice female newshound.

MARY: Is Alan bright? *(She is lighting the candle on the table.)*

JOSEPH: Eh?

MARY: You'd never say that about a man. Women aren't supposed to be bright so you have to comment on it.

JOSEPH: We only had a snack. *(And he flings out.)*

SANDY *comes in wearing jeans and a top; looks in the kitchen cupboard.* SANDY *goes up to her.*

GEORGINA: You haven't asked.

SANDY: Asked what?

GEORGINA *(coy)*: How we are today.

SANDY: I can see how you are. Lazy.

GEORGINA: We, Sandy.

SANDY: It's nothing to do with me. Haven't we got anything to drink?

GEORGINA: Of course it's to do with you. We're in this together.

SANDY: Some people are more in than others.

GEORGINA: You make me feel ill when you're vulgar, Sandra.

SANDY: You won't be hungry for your dinner, then, will you? *(Pause.)* What did your friend Len want?

GEORGINA: Just to say hello. He'd heard.

SANDY: Knitting pink or blue boottees, is he?

GEORGINA: He's only interested, being friendly.

SANDY: You bet.

GEORGINA: We've been through it all.

SANDY: We sure have, kid.

GEORGINA: Are you going to be childish all evening?

SANDY: 'Childish' is an unfortunate word, in the circumstances.

GEORGINA: Aggressive, then.

SANDY: He'll be round, regular as clockwork.

GEORGINA: No, he won't. Men don't care about babies like women do.

SANDY: We'll see. *(She gets up.)* I'm going out for a drink.

GEORGINA *(sarky)*: No, thanks. I'd rather stay in and meditate.

SANDY: Expect me when you see me.

She flings her jacket over her shoulder and goes out. GEORGINA shows signs of annoyance, then looks at her watch, gets up, takes the bottle of wine, her jacket and goes out as well.

JOSEPH back in, now clean and changed.

MARY: Aren't you wearing your blue shirt?

JOSEPH: You didn't iron my blue shirt.

MARY: Oh, God no, so I didn't.

JOSEPH: What do you want to drink?

MARY: We'll wait till they arrive. Don't want to mess things up.

JOSEPH: Mary, I'm tired.

MARY: Don't start doing your breadwinner routine now, Joe, I've got to see to the sprouts.

JOSEPH: Well, I'm off to get some more booze.

MARY: Don't be long?

JOSEPH: Expect me when you see me.

Scene Two

MARY left alone looks round to check the room, notices a tape measure on a chair, picks it up to tidy it away, then suddenly decides to measure her waist. Just as she does so, the bell rings. She takes her apron off, then is about to put the tape measure away when the bell rings again. Flummoxed she runs to answer the door, tape measure still in her hand. Hellos from off.

MARY *(coming in, followed by GEORGINA)*: Do come in.

GEORGINA: I hope I'm not late.

MARY: Oh, no, no. Joseph's just popped out for a tonic — I mean, for some tonic. Have you come over on your own?

GEORGINA: Sandy's just popped out as well.

Slight awkwardness, then GEORGINA *hands the bottle of wine over.*

MARY: Oh — lovely. Do sit down.

GEORGINA: Thanks.

MARY: You'll forgive me if I keep popping off to stir. Would you like a drink?

GEORGINA: Lovely.

MARY *(realises she still has the tape measure in her hand)*: Oh, silly me. I was just — measuring my waist. Silly, isn't it?

GEORGINA: Well, I don't — I mean —

MARY: Whatever turns you on?

GEORGINA: I mean, you're not actually harming anyone, are you?

MARY: It's just that it isn't something women are supposed to do nowadays. I was just tidying up and before I knew it — whip — there it was round my waist, and I was trying hard to be honest and not breathe in, so as to make it smaller than it was — you know —

GEORGINA: Er — yes —

MARY: Well, let's have drinkies, shall we? Martini? Whisky?

GEORGINA: Martini is fine.

MARY: I'm so glad you could both come over so soon. When we moved into the square we didn't get to know our neighbours for months, so I thought, this time I'll make the first move. Lemon?

GEORGINA: Thank you.

MARY *(brings drinks forward, then remembers)*: Oh, ice. *(Goes back to get it.)* I don't suppose you've met many people —

GEORGINA: Well, I used to live round the corner, so I know the area quite well.

MARY: Really? Well, you can probably tell me more than I can tell you.

GEORGINA: Oh, it was years ago.

MARY: Where have you been since?

GEORGINA: Manchester for the last five years.

MARY *(coming back with ice)*: Oh yes, I can detect just the teeniest twinge of an accent. It's just the two of you, is it?

GEORGINA: In the house? Yes, it is. At the moment.

MARY: I'm very curious about people. Nosy, Joe calls it. Joe's my husband. I expect you've seen him dashing in and out. He's a reporter on the local paper.

GEORGINA: Oh really?

MARY *(sits down beside* GEORGINA*)*: He's frightfully good at it, always digging up scandals. *(Pause.)* Now then. What do you do?

GEORGINA: I'm a photographer.

MARY: Oh, how glamorous. Now me, I absolutely adore being at home now. Ten years of tapping a typewriter was quite enough.

GEORGINA: Did you get tired of working?

MARY: Oh, I was always tired of working. No, I'm starting a baby. Well, Joe and me are starting a baby. It takes two, doesn't it?

GEORGINA: Oh, yes.

MARY: We decided it was time to start a family. I only stopped work last month, but there's so much to do in the house, isn't there? You don't notice it when you're out at work. I suppose that once I've got all the nappies and that, I shall be absolutely longing for my Tippex again.

GEORGINA: How pregnant are you?

MARY: Oh, good Lord, I'm not pregnant yet.

GEORGINA: Oh, I see.

MARY: We're been trying awfully hard but nothing's happened so far. Our doctor — he's a lovely man — he suggested I should give up work, relax a bit more, that might do the trick. *(Suddenly remembering and jumping up.)* Oh — I must do the dressing. *(She rushes off.)* Are you doing lots of work on the house?

GEORGINA *(getting up and looking round the room)*: We've had to have a damp course put in.

MARY: So that's what the banging is.

GEORGINA: I hope it's not disturbing you?

MARY: Not at all. I just like to know what it is I can hear. You know this was one big house when it was originally built. Yours and ours. It was divided down the middle — that's why some of the dividing walls are a bit — well — flimsy. Don't put any bookshelves up on them.

GEORGINA: Right. I'll remember that. You must come over and have a look round.

MARY: Oh, what a lovely idea. *(She drops half a lemon.)* Whoops. Clumsy clogs. Good thing it wasn't the garlic.

GEORGINA: Why's that?

MARY: Keeps the vampires away. I always carry one round in my bag. A clove of garlic, I mean, not a vampire.

GEORGINA: Does it work?

MARY: Of course. I've never been attacked by a vampire. *(Sound of front door opening.)* This must be him. Joe, I mean, not the vampire.

Enter JOSEPH, carrying a bag of drink. Over his entry.

He's had one of his hard days. You know how men are.

JOSEPH: 'Evening. Five tonics, two sodas and a partridge in a bottle of brandy for afters.

MARY: Joseph, this is Georgina Archer, from next door. Georgina, this is Joe, my husband. *(Stage whisper.)* Joe, please don't be hearty.

JOSEPH: You two girls been having a cosy gossip?

MARY: Women, Joe.

JOSEPH: Sorry — women. I love having a wife who's nearly a feminist.

MARY: Sarky.

JOSEPH: A demi-feminist, then. Nice to meet you, Georgina. *(He shakes hands with her.)*

GEORGINA: Hello. I can't think what's happened to Sandy.

JOSEPH: Which one of you rides the bike?

GEORGINA: Sandy.

MARY: Joe's always wanted a motorbike. I tell him that once we've got the baby, he won't want a motorbike any more.

JOSEPH: Mary has these sub-Freudian theories about men wanting babies as a substitute for the motorbike their Daddies didn't buy them. Sort of technological penis envy.

MARY: I do so love having a husband who's nearly an intellectual.

GEORGINA: Well, Sandy's the one for bikes. She's had one ever since we — er, ever since I've known her. I'm sorry she's so late.

MARY: A woman should never say she's sorry. Not any more.

JOSEPH *(from the back)*: Mary, are these brussel sprouts or roast chestnuts?

MARY *(leaping up)*: Oh, heavens. *(Calls as she goes off.)* Joe, the chairs.

JOE *puts four chairs round the table.*

GEORGINA: Mary says you work on the Gazette.

JOSEPH: That's right.

GEORGINA: I've just written to your editor.

JOSEPH: Oh yes, got a complaint?

GEORGINA: No — I've got some photographs —

MARY: Georgina's a photographer.

GEORGINA: I have some contacts at one of the local hospitals.

JOSEPH: Oh yes.

GEORGINA: A friend of mine's a nurse, and she's told me about the plan to merge two ante-natal clinics.

MARY: Oh, Joe knows all about that, don't you, darling? He's written at least one article on it.

JOSEPH: I was telling Mary earlier.

There is a ring at the front door.

MARY: I'll go.

JOSEPH: I was telling Mary about —

SANDY *enters, wearing plastic motorbike trousers, a leather bomber jacket, helmet and gauntlets.*

SANDY: Howdy, neighbours.

GEORGINA: Ah, this is Sandy — Sandra. Sandra, Joe and Mary. I'm sorry —

SANDY: Howdy. *(She takes off her helmet and hands it to* JOE.*)*

JOSEPH: Hello.

MARY *(who has followed* SANDY *in)*: We're so glad you could drop over.

SANDY: Pleased to meet you. *(She holds out a hand to shake, then notices she's still wearing the gloves, takes them off and hands them to* MARY.*)*

JOSEPH: Haven't I seen you somewhere before?

SANDY: You had three double whiskies in the public bar. Had a tiff with the missus, I thought. Just like me.

MARY: Well, shall we all sit down? Joseph, the wine.

JOSEPH: Yes, please sit down. Anywhere.

MARY: When the woman cooks the dinner, the man pours the wine. That's one thing that will never change.

GEORGINA: Sandy's sorry she's late.

SANDY: Sorry I was so late. Staff meeting in the pub.

GEORGINA: Sandy's a teacher.

JOSEPH: Is that your motorbike?

GEORGINA: Rather.

JOSEPH: I'm afraid I've been coveting it ever since you moved in.

SANDY: Have a go on it if you like.

MARY: Oh, Joe doesn't know how to ride. *(She has brought the first course in.)* I'm afraid the toast's a little burnt.

SANDY: Never mind. Charcoal's good for the blood.

JOSEPH: Actually, my Dad courted my Mum on a BSA in Epping Forest. I was born with engine oil in my blood.

MARY: Sounds nasty, doesn't it? *(To* SANDY.*)* So you're a teacher.

SANDY: About to get promoted, I trust. Eh, Georgie?

GEORGINA: Sandy's in line for the head of department.

JOSEPH: It's the new Honda, isn't it?

SANDY: CG125.

GEORGINA: She reads the catalogues in the loo.

SANDY: Toilet, dear.

JOSEPH: I fancy an Electra-Glide.

MARY: Sounds like hell on two wheels.

JOSEPH: Always wanted to be a Hell's Angel.

SANDY: A closet Hell's Angel, eh?

GEORGINA *kicks her under the table.*

MARY: Closet?

SANDY: Ow.

MARY: Is it too burnt?

SANDY: Closet is — well, when someone hides what they are, or keeps it very quiet for some reason. Like, say, you might have someone who appears to be homosexual, but is actually hetero in their head.

MARY: I'm afraid I don't follow — isn't it usually the other way round? I mean, I've read about it —

JOSEPH: Where do you teach?

SANDY: Middleside Comprehensive. It's a very progressive school.

GEORGINA: You should hear her on a bad day.

MARY: Oh, I expect we shall. Oh. I mean — well, I was telling Georgina — your house and ours used to be one big — and then it was divided in two, and — Joe, darling, help me with the plates, would you?

They go off into the kitchen.

GEORGINA: Cool it, Sandy, ok?

SANDY: Cool what, my love?

GEORGINA: You're behaving badly.

SANDY: Behaving? That's a very middle-class word.

GEORGINA: I'll tell them, then, shall I?

SANDY: Who? What?

GEORGINA: Help you come out of your closet. Spell it out in neon lights for you.

SANDY: Be as brave as you like in the privacy of your own home, can't you?

GEORGINA: Look, I'm not bothered. We can make this your coming out party, if you like. Right? Shall I tell them?

SANDY: Alright, keep your badges on.

MARY *and* JOSEPH *return with food.*

MARY: The sprouts are a little overdone, I'm afraid.

JOSEPH: How do you like living in the area?

SANDY: Oh, it's fine. We had a bit of trouble over the mortgage, but then George's father came up trumps and lent us the deposit.

MARY: George. That's rather an unusual nickname.

SANDY: After Enid Blyton and Beryl Reid. Five run away with Sister George.

GEORGINA: Although Sandy here teaches maths, she is an intrepid member of the local public library, and has been known to actually finish an entire book.

MARY: You know, you two remind me of when I shared a flat. Remember me and Annie, Joe?

JOSEPH: Er, more wine?

MARY: Always bickering we were, like an old married couple.

GEORGINA: Oh, Sandy, Mary and Joseph are going to have a baby.

JOSEPH: When we get pregnant.

MARY: Oh, Joe. When I get pregnant.

SANDY: Georgina likes babies.

MARY: Oh, wonderful.

SANDY: She has a fetish about ante-natal clinics. Can't seem to keep away from them.

MARY: Oh, yes. Your friend.

JOSEPH: Ah yes. The hospital.

MARY: Hospitals, schools; once you're pregnant, it's a whole new world. Is Middleside a good school?

SANDY: On the whole.

JOSEPH: That's looking ahead a bit, Mary.

MARY: Well, you have to plan, don't you.

GEORGINA: Sandy worked in a free school for a bit. Believed in the principles but couldn't stand the mess.

SANDY: I still believe in the principles. But people don't seem to have the enthusiasm they used to in the early seventies.

MARY: Gosh, you've known each other a long time.

JOSEPH: How did you handle the whole question of the relationship between free choice and responsibility?

MARY: Super. A political discussion.

GEORGINA: Sandy dealt with it very well. Used to come home with a migraine every day.

SANDY: Has Georgina told you about her squat?

MARY: Oh no. How decadent.

SANDY: Georgina comes from a wealthy family in Manchester. But being a socialist, she decided she ought to experience poverty.

MARY: And?

SANDY: Well, she kept the coal in the bath, and ran home to Mummy to use the spin-dryer.

MARY: I think we're all going to get on splendidly.

Scene Three

GEORGINA *and* JOSEPH *get into their respective beds.* GEORGINA *lies down to go to sleep,* JOSEPH *settles down to read* Spare Rib. MARY *gets into bed, with a selection of midnight blue baby's sweaters.*

Focus on GEORGINA's *half.* SANDY *sits on the side of the bed, starts putting cream on her face, humming* 'I'm gonna wash that man right out of my hair'. *She leans over onto* GEORGINA *rather heavily to reach a box of tissues.* GEORGINA *flounces up.*

GEORGINA: Alright, Sandy, you've made your point. Now keep bloody still.

SANDY: I don't know what you're talking about.

GEORGINA: Look, he's a friend, he only did it to oblige.

SANDY: Because he knows it pleases.

GEORGINA: Oh, shut up.

SANDY: Well, what's important is that you should be happy about it. Calm and contented.

GEORGINA: Sandy, do you want me to get rid of it?

SANDY: Perish the thought.

GEORGINA: We decided together, remember?

SANDY: Yup.

GEORGINA: Oh, you make me sick.

SANDY: What, at this time of night. Early morning is when you're supposed to feel nauseous.

GEORGINA *flings herself under the covers and* SANDY *gets in beside her.*

JOSEPH *and* MARY's *bed.* JOSEPH *puts his magazine away.*

JOSEPH: Come on, Mary.

MARY: I think I'll do another two jackets and then I can start on the nighties.

JOSEPH: What, now?

MARY: No, silly.

JOSEPH: Isn't it cheaper at Mothercare?

MARY: You're joking. Anyway, it's not the money that counts. It's the love that goes into it. They're nice, aren't they?

JOSEPH: Lovely. I hope it likes navy blue.

MARY: Midnight, Joe. No, I mean Sandy and Georgina.

JOSEPH: Mmmm.

MARY: I'm sorry about the brussel sprouts.

JOSEPH: They are nice.

MARY: When they're properly cooked.

JOSEPH: Sandy and Georgina?

MARY: Brussel sprouts. They're very liberated, aren't they?

JOSEPH: Brussel sprouts?

MARY: Sandy and Georgina. Joe.

JOSEPH: Mmmm.

MARY: Why do you want a baby?

JOSEPH: Now she asks me. To leave my mortgage and overdraft to.

MARY: Seriously.

JOSEPH: Why do you?

MARY: Same reason as any other woman. All the same reasons. Because I want to. But it's not the same for a man, is it?

JOSEPH: No. I'll never know what it's actually like to have it.

MARY: How amazing.

JOSEPH: Why?

MARY: I'll never understand men.

GEORGINA *(sitting up)*: Sandy.

SANDY *(stirring)*: What's wrong, love? D'you feel sick?

GEORGINA: Sandy. Wake up.

SANDY: Come on, I'll come with you.

GEORGINA: No, Sandy, look. *(She pushes back the bedclothes, to reveal a blood-stained sheet.)*

SANDY: Oh, Christ. I'll ring the hospital.

Scene Four

Early morning. MARY *stirs in bed, starts to sit up.* JOSEPH *jumps up.*

JOSEPH: Oh, no you don't.

He grabs a thermometer from the side of the bed and puts it in her mouth to stop the following line.

MARY: I want a cup of tea.

JOSEPH: Shut up. *(He looks at his watch, then takes the thermometer out to read it.)* Thirty-seven point two, thirty-seven point three, thirty-seven point four — going up — thirty-seven point five. *(Triumph.)* Second day running. *(He puts the thermometer away and marks the reading on a chart pinned to the wall by the bed. Then he puts a ring round the last reading.)* Right. On your back, girl.

MARY: I'm fed up with the missionary position.

JOSEPH: It's for our own good, my love.

MARY: When we're pregnant, I'll be on top every time.

JOSEPH: Promises, promises.

MARY: Have you done a circle?

JOSEPH: I have indeed indicated intercourse on post-ovulatory days.

MARY: Oh, Joe, you say the sweetest things.

JOSEPH: I hope my language doesn't take all the fun out of it.

MARY: Don't you believe it.

Music; 'Goodnight, Sweetheart'.

Scene Five

MARY's *half*

MARY: I'm sure it's for the best in the long run. I mean, there must have been something wrong or it wouldn't have happened, would it? I mean, how on earth would you have managed?

GEORGINA: Sandy and me had it all worked out.

MARY: But what about the — well, you know — the —

GEORGINA: There wasn't one.

MARY: Wasn't one what?

GEORGINA: You mean the father?

MARY: Ah. I see. He doesn't care.

GEORGINA: No, he doesn't.

MARY: Men.

GEORGINA: No, it's not like that. I mean, he doesn't care because it isn't anything to do with him.

MARY: Just like a man. Do you know, there are times when I get so — angry — when if there was a way to join women's lib, I would join it — them, I mean. I'm as passionate as anyone about women's rights — mostly I think you have to take things nice and slow, but at times like this, and even though some of my best friends are men — well, I married one, didn't I? — at times like this I think the whole lot of them should be — oh, given a good hiding.

GEORGINA: He was only doing me a favour.

MARY: A favour?

GEORGINA: Yes. I wanted a baby. We both wanted a baby.

MARY: Then he should stand by you. It's just like a man to run out on his responsibilities.

GEORGINA: Sandy and me wanted a baby. Len helped us out.

MARY: Sandy?

GEORGINA: Len's an old friend.

MARY: Didn't he care?

GEORGINA: Well, no, not particularly.

MARY: It sounds so — clinical.

GEORGINA: It was quite a laugh really. You know, forging new frontiers. Sandy got a bit upset. Maybe I'm being punished for it.

MARY: Oh, don't be silly. Even royalty miscarries.

GEORGINA: Anyway, I won't ask Len again.

MARY: Georgina, I hope you won't mind my asking. I mean, I am a bit — frank — well, I do pride myself on being very open-minded about things — life — and what I, well, you and Sandy, next door — do you, I mean, are you — well, I'm sure you'll be very shocked if the answer's no, just like I'll be very shocked if the answer's yes — but what I would really like to know is —

GEORGINA: Sandy and me are lovers, yes.

MARY: Well, yes, I was quite right, I am shocked.

GEORGINA: Here, shall I make you some tea?

MARY: Yes, please, very strong.

GEORGINA: I'm sure it's not as though you disapprove.

MARY: It isn't as though I disapprove.

GEORGINA: It's more that you've probably never knowingly had a lesbian in the house, let alone entertained a couple round to dinner — Earl Grey or PG Tips? — let alone consoled one after she's had a miscarriage.

MARY: Yes, well, I think you've put that rather well. Er, PG Tips.

GEORGINA: I mean, I look quite normal, don't I?

MARY: You do, yes.

GEORGINA: And Sandy's a terrific and very responsible teacher. All the kids like her.

MARY: I'm sure they do.

GEORGINA: And we're very committed to each other, aren't we, we have rows, just like real people.

MARY: Oh yes, the other night, you and Sandy were really going — oh, dear.

GEORGINA: And there's no need for us to leave visiting cards saying 'Sandy and Georgina are Lesbians', is there?

MARY: Good heavens no, what a ridiculous idea.

GEORGINA: I mean, if we had, you might have thought twice about having us round for dinner, mightn't you? Not because you're prejudiced, of course —

MARY: No, but one has to think these things out.

GEORGINA: But now you can see that we're not really very different from the rest of your friends, it's all quite alright, isn't it? I mean, you were absolutely right not to hold any prejudice against us.

MARY: Georgina, I do believe you're trying to put words into my mouth.

Scene Six

SANDY *and* GEORGINA *sitting up in bed.*

SANDY: Georgie.

GEORGINA: Mmm.

SANDY: I'm sorry, love.

GEORGINA: Eh? Have you done something I haven't noticed?

SANDY: Sorry I was such a pig.

GEORGINA: Gosh, Sand, you were a rotter and a swine.

SANDY: I mean about Len.

GEORGINA: Ah.

SANDY: I didn't mean it.

GEORGINA: Of course you did.

SANDY: Of course I did.

Pause.

GEORGINA: Sandy.

SANDY: Mmm.

GEORGINA: What shall we do?

SANDY: What do you want to do?

GEORGINA: I still want to have a baby.

SANDY: There's still only one way of having one.

GEORGINA: It's not on, is it, Sand?

SANDY: Perhaps we could adopt one.

GEORGINA: Who would let us adopt a baby?

SANDY: It's been known.

GEORGINA: No. I want to have one. Myself.

SANDY: Well, I don't know, Georgie. Maybe it's all impossible.

GEORGINA: You're not changing your mind?

SANDY: I don't think so. But for once in my life, I haven't got all the answers.

GEORGINA: Where there's a will, there's got to be a way.

SANDY: No, Georgie, love. Willpower doesn't make you pregnant.

Scene Seven

JOSEPH *and* MARY *asleep in bed.* MARY *wakes suddenly. Sits up.*

MARY: I think you'd better start carving the cradle.

JOSEPH: Eh?

MARY: And buy a donkey. A white one.

JOSEPH: Have you got a temperature?

MARY: I had that dream again. This hippie, dressed like a medieval pilgrim, sitting on the end of the bed, whispering: 'Mon nam is Geoffroi Chaucer; whan that you a mothre wille bee, youre happinesse wille shine like the sunne . . .'

JOSEPH: Delusions of immaculacy, Mary love. Forget it. We'll have to put our faith in science.

MARY: Only last night he didn't sound Middle English. He sounded Middle European.

JOSEPH: Sigmund Freud in the comfort of our own home. Look, love, you'll have to stop reading Spare Rib. It's giving you pretensions beyond your intellect.

MARY: Joe.

JOSEPH: Not now, Mary. I've got a low on my bio-rhythms.

MARY: What time will you be home tomorrow?

JOSEPH: Tomorrow?

MARY: I've got to plan the meal. Chicken Sauté Bourgignonne.

JOSEPH: And brussel sprouts?

MARY: Braised mangetout. Practice is making me a perfect cook.

JOSEPH: Immaculacy — perfection — where will it all end.

MARY: Maybe I could *dream* us into pregnancy.

Scene Eight

JOSEPH *and* MARY's *bed. The doctor stands by the bed. As soon as she starts to speak*, JOSEPH *and* MARY *sit up*.

DOCTOR: I know statistics are not necessarily consoling in themselves, but it is estimated that one couple in six is unable to conceive. I have read both your notes and it seems to me that before we proceed with more drastic measures, we should try AIH.

JOSEPH: Eh?

DOCTOR: That's right. AIH. Artificial Insemination by Husband.

JOSEPH: How does that work?

DOCTOR: Well, we're not really sure why that should work when normal intercourse doesn't, but I think it is well worth trying.

MARY: And if it doesn't work?

DOCTOR: Well, we could do some surgical exploration, see whether your Fallopian tubes are blocked; sometimes very gently stretching the neck of the womb helps receptivity to spermatozoa, and there is of course, AID.

MARY: What's that?

DOCTOR: Well, let me put it to you this way. If your chicken doesn't lay eggs, you can always change the cock.

JOSEPH: I beg your pardon?

DOCTOR: Just my little joke. Sometimes it puts people at their ease. I mean simply, Artificial Insemination by Donor.

JOSEPH: Another man?

DOCTOR: Yes.

JOSEPH: Mary, what a way to break it to me.

MARY: Joe — I —

DOCTOR: No, no, no, you don't understand. I mean a healthy male donor, whose sperm motility count is higher than your own, who remains anonymous, and who would be chosen for his matching physical type to yourself.

JOSEPH: How could I be sure it wasn't my next-door neighbour?

MARY: It's hardly likely, Joe.

DOCTOR: We're very careful about that sort of thing. Anyway, we don't have to make any decision about that just yet. Now, would you like to go ahead with AIH?

JOSEPH: Mary? How do you fancy fucking by proxy?

MARY: It's worth a try, eh?

JOSEPH: I never thought you'd commit adultery with a test-tube.

Scene Nine

The doctor stands by SANDY *and* GEORGINA*'s bed. As soon as she starts to speak,* SANDY *and* GEORGINA *sit up.*

DOCTOR: Well, physically you're fine now and there's no reason why you shouldn't go ahead.

SANDY: What exactly is involved.

DOCTOR: It's very simple and in a few years it will probably become quite widely accepted as a form of treatment for infertility.

GEORGINA: There's no risk of the man having VD or anything?

DOCTOR: Good heavens, no. We check the health credentials of our donors far more carefully than any married couple check each other. If you have preferences as to physiological type, we will try and fill them. All our donors are young professional men, doctors, medical students, even journalists sometimes. I'm afraid I can't guarantee the sex of the baby.

GEORGINA: And it's all anonymous.

DOCTOR: And confidential.

SANDY: What's the legal status?

DOCTOR: You're simply an unmarried mother. No problems. No problems, that is, apart from those which unmarried mothers have. Well?

SANDY: We'll think about it.

GEORGINA: Thank you, Doctor.

Scene Ten

The next scenes are played from offstage, so the audience sees nothing. If the stage is the right size and shape, two areas, near the beds, can have hospital screens, behind which the scenes take place.

Screen 1

NURSE: Now. The bottle's got quite a wide neck, so you should be quite alright. Have you abstained from intercourse for the last few days?

JOSEPH: Er — yes.

NURSE: Well, I'll just leave you to it. Take your time. There's plenty of magazines there if you want them — Penthouse, New Statesman. Sometimes they help.

JOSEPH: No thanks. I'll just lie back and think of England.

Screen 2

NURSE: There you are. That's all it is. Now, you can take your time, no-one
will disturb you. You may like to — use the bed — you know. Stay on the
bed for about twenty minutes after the insemination with your legs up — put
the syringe in the bin when you've finished. Alright?

SANDY
GEORGINA *(together)*: Yes, thanks.

SANDY: Well, my love, up you get.

Sounds of GEORGINA *climbing onto the bed.*

GEORGINA *(mock Mae West)*: Come up and join me sometime.

SANDY *is heard trying to climb up on the bed, which is long and narrow, she
is then heard falling off, to the sound of a great deal of giggling.*

GEORGINA: It's no good, Sandy, you'll just have to be clinical about it.

SANDY: In all my struggles against monogamy in the nuclear couple, I never
thought I would aid and abet you to be unfaithful to me with a plastic
syringe.

GEORGINA: Isn't science wonderful?

Screen 1

NURSE: There you are, Mrs Lacey. Getting to be quite a regular now. What
is it, third try?

MARY: Yes, I'm afraid so.

NURSE: Husband not here today?

MARY: He had to go to work, he couldn't stay.

NURSE: Comfortable?

MARY: As can be expected.

NURSE: Well, I'll pop back in about twenty minutes. Got enough magazines?

MARY: I'll just read my book.

NURSE: Nuisance, isn't it? Never mind, maybe this time you'll strike gold.

Screen 2

NURSE: Mrs Archer. Ah, take a seat, Mrs Archer.

GEORGINA: Not Mrs.

NURSE: Pardon?

GEORGINA: Not Mrs Archer. I'm Ms Archer.

NURSE: Yes, well, here at the ante-natal clinic we call all the Mums 'Mrs'.
Saves embarrassment all round. Now, let's fill in this form, shall we? Age?

GEORGINA: Thirty-three.

NURSE: Oh dear. First baby?

GEORGINA: Yes.

NURSE: Father?

GEORGINA: Don't know.

NURSE: Do you live alone?

GEORGINA: With a friend.

NURSE: Dear oh dear. Well. Given your advancing years and your unstable home situation, you may well have to be induced. And you will certainly have to stay in hospital for the full ten days. At least. Now, collect your vitamin and iron pills and then you'd better go and see the social worker.

GEORGINA: Social worker?

NURSE: To discuss having it adopted.

GEORGINA: I'm not having it adopted.

NURSE: I see. You'll be telling me next you got pregnant on purpose.

Scene Eleven

SANDY*'s half.* SANDY *comes on with a pile of exercise books, squats down on the cushions and begins marking.* JOSEPH *comes in, knocking on the door as he does so.*

SANDY: Hello

JOSEPH: Er — hello — er — *(He looks round.)*

SANDY: Looking for Georgie?

JOSEPH: She's supposed to give me some photos.

SANDY: Oh. Well, I don't know where she is. *(Looks round, then sees an envelope.)* Ah — look in that, that looks like photos.

JOSEPH *(takes envelope and looks)*: Yes. This looks like it.

He hangs around, a bit awkward.

SANDY: Hang on and wait for her if you like.

JOSEPH: Thanks. Didn't hear the bike today.

SANDY: It's been wheezing like Walter Gabriel. I spent all yesterday on it and gave up.

JOSEPH: Listen, would you show me how to ride it? Give Mary a surprise.

SANDY: Sure. *(Awkward pause, during which they both start talking at once, then* SANDY *wins.)* Want a drink?

JOSEPH: Er — no thanks.

SANDY: Are those the right photos?

JOSEPH: They look fine. She's not a bad photographer.

SANDY: I'll tell her. She likes a nice compliment. *(Pause.)* How is Mary?

JOSEPH: Oh, fine, fine.

SANDY: Hit the jackpot yet?

JOSEPH: Pardon? Oh. Oh, I see. Well, no, actually.

SANDY: Sorry. Just making conversation.

JOSEPH: No, no that's quite alright. I mean, I sometimes think Mary and me should invite everyone round to watch. I should think there's more people know how high my sperm count is than know my middle name.

SANDY: What's your middle name?

JOSEPH: I haven't got one.

SANDY: Ah.

JOSEPH: My sperm motility — if you really want to know — is below average. That is, only about fifty percent of the little beasts are alive and kicking. Well, wiggling. Imagine, only half of five or six hundred million of them alive. You know, I sometimes think there's some fault in the engineering. Talk about over-production. I don't suppose you're very interested.

SANDY: Well, I have an interest in the mechanics of life, even if it is rather academic.

JOSEPH: You know, if we had a choice, there's nothing I'd rather do than have our baby. Then I could fertilise it myself and — hey presto.

SANDY: God, I wouldn't.

JOSEPH: Wouldn't what?

SANDY: Want to have a baby myself. I'd feel I was being invaded.

JOSEPH: Don't you want a baby?

SANDY: Oh, I'm really looking forward to having a kid around. And Georgie — she hasn't been so excited about anything since we queued in Birmingham to see 'South Pacific'. Here, have you ever said that to a man?

JOSEPH: What?

SANDY: That thing about wanting to have a baby.

JOSEPH: God, no. Can you imagine. They'd all make jokes about me wanting to change sex — limp wrists held up at me when I go into the pub — *(He suddenly realises.)* Oh, look, I'm terribly sorry — I didn't mean to —

SANDY: It's alright, I'm not offended. I'm sorry it's a problem for you.

JOSEPH: Oh, it's not a problem. Not a problem as such.

SANDY: But the thought of other men thinking you want to be a woman makes you feel a bit — paranoid?

JOSEPH: One is only paranoid insofar as one is being actually persecuted. Well, I must be going.

SANDY: Sure you don't want to wait for Georgie?

JOSEPH: No, thanks. Got something to finish off. See you.

SANDY: 'Bye.

JOSEPH *exits;* SANDY *continues marking.*

JOSEPH enters his own house, goes to the desk and sits down to the typewriter. He begins typing. GEORGINA *enters her home at the same time as* MARY *enters hers.*

GEORGINA *(coming to kiss SANDY)*: Hello, love.

MARY *(coming to kiss JOSEPH)*: Hello, darling.

JOSEPH: Hello. Good film?

MARY: Lovely. Georgie came with me.

SANDY: Good film?

GEORGINA: Terrific. Mary came with me.

MARY: Joe, you must see it. She delivered the whole baby herself, with those really nice nurses, and they were all smiling and making jokes, and you should have seen the baby's face — it was such a scrawny little thing —

GEORGINA: I'm going to see it again.

SANDY: Great. I'll come with you.

MARY: Joe.

JOSEPH: Mmm?

MARY: Georgina's pregnant.

JOSEPH: Mary. Terrific. Why didn't you tell me sooner?

MARY: I was saving it to tell you with the After Eights.

JOSEPH *(knocks on the dividing wall twice)*: Georgie, hey, Georgie.

SANDY *(to GEORGINA)*: It's for you.

GEORGINA *gets up and knocks twice in reply.*

JOSEPH *(knocks three times)*: Come over.

GEORGINA *knocks once in reply, then beckons to SANDY and the two of them go out.*

JOSEPH: You know, I was only talking to Sandy a few minutes ago and she didn't say anything — Oh, Mary, love, I am sorry.

MARY: It's not your fault. It just seems a bit unfair.

Ring at the bell. JOSEPH *goes to answer the door. He returns, followed by* DAPHNE.

MARY: Daphne. How lovely to see you. Where on earth have you been?

DAPHNE: Here, there, everywhere. Mainly there. Didn't old Joe say I was coming round?

MARY: No, he didn't, Joe, you horror, why didn't you tell me?

JOSEPH: I was saving her for the After Eights.

MARY: So what are you doing in London.

DAPHNE: I've come home.

MARY: You're reading the news for the BBC?

DAPHNE: Don't be silly, they've got their quota of female voices for the news. Local radio.

MARY: Great, that's really great.

JOSEPH: I ran into her in the pub. You know, all journalist chaps together.

DAPHNE: He's still a liberal, isn't he?

MARY: Yes. Maybe being a father will change that. They don't call having a baby 'labour' for nothing, do they?

DAPHNE: Mary — congratulations. *(To* JOE.*)* I knew you'd do it.

JOSEPH: Well, we've done it — but we haven't done it yet, in a manner of speaking. How's Lucy?

DAPHNE: Great. Comprehensive next year. I'm thinking of sending her to Middleside. Do you know anything about it?

MARY: Don't tell him all the news — I'll make some coffee. *(And she goes to the back to make coffee.)*

JOSEPH: Our neighbour teaches at Middleside; she can tell you more than I can.

MARY: Where are you staying?

DAPHNE: I'm staying with my Auntie Ivy. She sends her love. Joe, Lucy's playing bridge now.

JOSEPH: You can bring her round for a game, then.

DAPHNE *(noticing the list)*: Joe, what's this?

JOSEPH: That's our list of baby-sitters.

DAPHNE: Eh?

JOSEPH: For when we need to call on them. In time.

DAPHNE: All men.

JOSEPH: This is a progressive household. Oh, that reminds me. *(He crosses a name off.)* Greg's moved to Leeds.

SANDY *and* GEORGINA *come in.*

JOSEPH: May I introduce you to —

SANDY: Daphne, you cow, you never answered my letters.

DAPHNE: Sandy — your hair — hey, you've come out at last.

GEORGINA: No, she hasn't, she's going to be a sleek model when she grows up.

MARY *brings the tray down to the coffee table.*

MARY: Joe, I think they know each other.

JOSEPH: I gather, Daphne, you are already acquainted with our new neighbours?

DAPHNE: Sandy? Sandy your new neighbour? Have you got squatters in?

GEORGINA: We've bought the house next door, Sandy and me.

DAPHNE: You've been and gone respectable. Oh, you disappoint me.

SANDY: Wifey here's in the club.

JOSEPH: Georgie, well done.

DAPHNE: Georgie pregnant? Sandy, you old devil, you had the operation after all.

SANDY: Oh, it was nothing. Really.

GEORGINA: Our house is exactly the same as this.

DAPHNE: What, just for you two?

GEORGINA: Well, now we've started, who knows where it will all end? We'll give you a guided tour later.

DAPHNE: Well, this is something. Sandy, Joe was the guy I told you about, on the Llanelli Post.

SANDY: He can't be.

DAPHNE: He must have changed. Matured. Eh, Joe?

JOSEPH: Like many men today, Daphne, I prefer to draw a fine mist over the deeds of my past.

DAPHNE: In those days he liked wining and dining a young apprentice journalist before discussing possible promotion.

JOSEPH: Yes, well, we're all a lot older now.

DAPHNE: You know, it was him made me into a feminist. Reporting Saturday weddings and then fighting off his convictions that he was Robert Redford. Still, as you say, we're all a lot older now.

MARY *(indicating tray)*: Who's going to be mother?

DAPHNE: Sandy. (SANDY *doesn't look impressed.*)

GEORGINA: Well, now you've heard our good news, here is the bad news.

MARY: Oh, no, Sandy.

SANDY: Oh yes. I heard today.

GEORGINA: I think she should appeal.

SANDY: You can't appeal. It's a fair competition.

JOSEPH: Did they give you any reason?

SANDY: No. Form letter saying how much they regretted they couldn't offer me the job, and a note from the head saying it was a close thing, and he was sure I'd work well with the new man.

MARY *(to DAPHNE)*: Sandy's head of department retired.

SANDY: I did have a plan. I thought I would go in to the headmaster and say: 'Good morning, Mr Fatty, thank you for not making me head of maths because I am a nasty perverted lesbian dyke and everyone knows or suspects it, but daren't really say anything about it because I'm so terribly good at my job, and it's largely because of me that this school has such a high rate of numeracy among its pupils, and I know that Mr James, who did get the job, has also got a family — and eleven hundred cc's — to support — but it is true, isn't it, that the only reason I didn't get it was because I'm a lesbian.' But I thought better of it. No point losing my job as well.

GEORGINA: You can see she hasn't come out, can't you?

SANDY: There's out and out.

DAPHNE: I hope it's not a rude question — ?

GEORGINA: AID.

DAPHNE: Well, I'll go to the top of our stairs.

JOSEPH: Whatever turns you on.

DAPHNE: You know why I'm here? No, of course, you can't possibly know why I'm here.

MARY: To renew acquaintances.

DAPHNE: Well, yes. But also. Do you know who Geraldine Kramer is?

JOSEPH: Wasn't she the woman who tried to get male nudes on page three of the Telegraph?

DAPHNE: No, but it sounds as though you're getting warm.

SANDY: She wrote an article on teenagers, saying that the pill leads to schoolgirl nymphomania.

MARY: Really, Joe?

JOSEPH: Nonsense, scaremongering.

DAPHNE: So that's what Ms Geraldine Kramer has been up to. Well, here's what she's planning to get up to. This, my friends, is dynamite. Disturbing, provocative, dangerous, horrific, unnatural and immoral dynamite.

JOSEPH *(to* SANDY*)*: How long have you known young Daphne?

SANDY: Oh, about five years. She used to be in my women's group, way back. She's always liked being stage centre.

JOSEPH: I suppose if we let her rabbit on, she'll come to the point eventually?

SANDY: Bound to.

DAPHNE: Have you two finished?

JOSEPH: Have we?

SANDY: Oh, yes.

DAPHNE: Right. I'd like your reactions to the following outline for a series of three articles. Code name: 'Operation Dyke'.

The others snap into attention as a cod audience, producing puppet responses, where necessary. DAPHNE *refers to notes.*

Part One: A Family Opinion Poll, based on a random sample of the British population. Questions for the man in the street — (*To the others.*) — or should it be the woman on the streets? — on the great British family. Is it falling apart as a result of the massive social change of the last thirty years and the strident propaganda of women's lib?

They all shake their heads vehemently.

Or is it as solid as ever?

They all nod their heads vehemently.

Part Two: 'The thin end of the wedge'. It has come to my concerned attention that there are a number of doctors offering lesbians artificial insemination by donor. It seems to me that this is not simply an attempt by some isolated social misfits to normalise themselves as women by having babies, but possibly has more sinister motives behind it.

JOSEPH *(heckles)*: The CIA.

GEORGINA *(heckles)*: KGB.

MARY *(heckles)*: IBM.

DAPHNE: With your approval, I propose to offer myself as a guinea-pig in the interests of investigative journalism. I propose to dress up as a lesbian, infiltrate their secret organisations, purporting to be seeking access to artificial insemination. I will frequent such haunts as pubs, discos and, if necessary, political meetings of the left, where it is known that social deviants can take temporary refuge.

Applause.

I must stress the need for absolute secrecy. I shall be picking my way through a moral and ethical minefield.

SANDY: Daphne always had a wonderful imagination.

DAPHNE: Part Three: Comment from moral and spiritual leaders: interviews with Norman St John Stevas, Mary Whitehouse, Rhodes Boyson and the new Pope, if the paper is prepared to fly me out to Rome.

SANDY *(taking paper)*: It would be dishonest to pretend I had no bias myself. In my experience the popular and widespread myth of lesbians as two sweet old ladies, living a chintzy life in the country, feeding stray cats, is very far from the truth. The reality is that lesbian relationships, and I have seen a number in my profession, are more violent, tempestuous and fraught with jealousy, than any heterosexual relationship you can imagine. But naturally I will not let this subjective bias affect my professional objectivity.

DAPHNE: 'Sales potential . . .' Oh, I won't bother with that. Well?

GEORGINA: Not very, thank you.

SANDY: It's real?

JOSEPH: Does she know you've got it?

DAPHNE: Do me a favour.

JOSEPH: Where did you get it?

MARY: Someone ought to sort her out, paint slogans on her front door.

DAPHNE: Since when have you gone in for direct political action?

JOSEPH: Daphne —

DAPHNE: Yes, sorry, where did I get it. Well, having been out of town for a while, I've been racing round getting all my contacts oiled. Anyway, I did an article on rural communities in Wales, and I delivered it to the 'Daily Voice' — *(General noises of being impressed, which she acknowledges.)* — and while waiting for my commissioning editor to return from lunch, I was just casually looking through a pile of files and there was one marked 'Confidential'.

MARY: Daphne.

DAPHNE: So naturally I photocopied everything in it.

JOSEPH: Didn't anyone see you?

DAPHNE: No-one in the office.

JOSEPH: She will, as Mary says, have to be sorted out.

DAPHNE: And then — you'll never guess what.

They all lean forward, wrapt, and chorus 'What?'

She lives round the corner from my Auntie Ivy.

GEORGINA: What's that got to do with it?

DAPHNE: Nothing. Just thought you'd like to know.

SANDY: I don't like her plan. I don't like her plan at all.

MARY: There's a lot of people won't like her little plan.

DAPHNE: Well, my friends, seeing as how this has turned out to be quite a reunion, my wits are whizzing round like a Catherine wheel. Indeed, I might almost say a scheme is starting to germinate. Gather round, little children.

And she gathers them all into a group, their heads together, as the lights fade and Alma Cogan sings 'Hernando's Hideaway'.

ACT TWO

Scene One

Six weeks later. GEORGINA *enters wearing the apron* MARY *has worn in the first scene of the play, over a feminine dress. She is five months pregnant. She looks round the room with pleasure.*

DAPHNE *(sticks her head round the door)*: Anyone home?

GEORGINA: Daphne — what on earth —

DAPHNE *(enters, followed by* GERALDINE, *wearing appropriate casual be-jeaned gear with badges)*: 'Evening. Georgie. May I introduce Geraldine — Geraldine Marshall, Georgina Archer.

GEORGINA: Oh, hello. So glad you could come round. *(During the whole of this scene* GEORGINA *enacts an ultra-feminine role.)*

GERALDINE *(carrying a bottle of wine and wearing a large shoulder bag)*: Hello. So kind of you to invite me.

GEORGINA: Oh, that's alright. As soon as Sandy told me about you, I said, we must invite her round. Do you go to the disco every Friday? I don't bother much myself now . . . *(She pats her tum.)* Do let me take your jacket.

GERALDINE *hands her jacket over.*

Daphne, you will stay and have a nibble with us?

DAPHNE: No, thanks. I — er — bumped into Geraldine on the corner — so I thought I'd give her a lift. Got to dash and collect Lucy. *(To* GERALDINE.*)* Lucy's my daughter.

GERALDINE: Oh, I didn't know you were married.

DAPHNE: I'm not. Well, I'll love you and leave you.

GEORGINA: 'Bye, Daphne.

GERALDINE: Thanks for the lift.

DAPHNE: Any time. *(As she is about to exit, she bumps into* SANDY, *carrying a carrier bag with drink.)*

SANDY: Who's the road-block. Daphne, you old boot —

She suddenly notices GERALDINE *and comes sweeping in to greet her.* SANDY *is wearing a fitted man's dinner suit, stiff white cravat and a velvet bow tie.*

SANDY: Hello, there, Geraldine.

GERALDINE: Hello again.

SANDY: Daffers, park yourself and swig a drinkie. Didn't know you knew young Geraldine. *(Throughout this scene* SANDY *plays the 'male' role of the 'huntin', shootin', fishin' lesbian'.)*

GERALDINE: We live round the corner from each other.

DAPHNE: Well, must go and get Lucy. Love you and leave you.

She goes.

SANDY: Like my gear, Geraldine?

GERALDINE: It's quite marvellous.

SANDY: Took me weeks to find this tie. Only wear it at home, you understand.

GEORGINA: Sandy.

SANDY: Oh, sorry me old butch — er — Dutch. *(She hands the carrier bag over to* GEORGINA*.).*

GERALDINE: Oh — I brought some wine — I hope white's alright?

SANDY *(takes it, looks at it)*: '76, eh? Not a bad year, though perhaps a trifle young.

MARY *comes tripping in, carrying an empty cup.*

MARY: Anyone home?

SANDY: Liberty hall in here.

MARY: Oh. Didn't know you had guests.

SANDY: Geraldine, this is our neighbour Mary. Mary this is Geraldine — Marshall, friend of ours.

MARY: Oh gosh. How do you do? Are you one as well?

GERALDINE: Pardon?

MARY: I mean, a journalist.

GERALDINE: Yes, I am actually.

MARY: How fascinating. Who do you write for?

GERALDINE: I'm freelance. I write mainly for an American newspaper.

MARY: Sort of — co-respondent. I get all the jargon from my husband.

GEORGINA: Well, shall we have a drink?

MARY: Heavens, I nearly forgot. Georgina, may I borrow some Demerara raw cane sugar? I'm making damson preserve.

GEORGINA: Of course. Excuse me, Geraldine, while I just pop off and stir something. *(And she and* MARY *trip off lightly into the kitchen.)*

SANDY: Geraldine, do make yourself at home. Here, have a nut.

GERALDINE: Thanks. It's a lovely room.

SANDY: Georgie. Dab hand with the paintbrush.

GERALDINE: How long have you lived here?

SANDY: Moved in a few months ago. Time to settle down, we thought. You know.

From the back the sound of something dropping.

MARY *(off)*: Oh, I'm sorry, Georgina. Was it your last packet?

GEORGINA *(off)*: Don't worry.

SANDY *(has poured drinks, takes one over to* GERALDINE*)*: Now. Cheers, Geraldine. To Lesbos.

GEORGINA *(coming in)*: Oh, Sandy, you louse, you're drinking to Lesbos without me.

SANDY: To you and Lesbos, George.

MARY *(coming in with her cup of sugar)*: Well, I'll be off then.

SANDY: Happy cooking.

MARY *goes.* GEORGINA *goes back out, to kitchen.*

Did you see her?

GERALDINE: Yes. Your neighbour, is she?

SANDY: She is. She has had enormous problems adjusting to us, has Mary. But she's coming up trumps. Did you notice, George, she didn't blush once. Top up? *(She fills up* GERALDINE*'s glass.)* A woman's right to booze, eh? No, she's a lovely neighbour. Very unhappy, though.

GERALDINE: Oh? Why's that?

SANDY: Tragic. Hubby can't get her in the club. And us next door merrily gettin' on with it.

GERALDINE: Do they know what's wrong?

GEORGINA *(who has popped back in to get a spice jar)*: They haven't really found out yet. *(And she trips back out again.)*

GERALDINE: There's a lot that can be done now to help infertile couples.

SANDY: As we know, eh? Don't worry, we'll get on to chapter and verse all in good time.

GEORGINA *(calls from the back)*: Sand, help me open this jar.

SANDY *(gestures of 'helpless little woman')*: Coming, Georgie petal.

She goes off. GERALDINE *is briefly alone. She looks round, opens her bag, lifts out a tape recorder, switches it on, and checks the sound levels.* SANDY *returns just as she is closing the bag.*

GERALDINE: It really is a beautiful room. You've bought the house, have you? Just the two of you?

SANDY: Until the patter of tiny feet. Are you a Londoner?

GERALDINE: Basically. I've spent a lot of time abroad. Australia.

GEORGINA *(popping back in to replace the jar)*: Oh, I thought I could detect just the teeniest twinge of an accent. *(And she pops out again. During this next section* SANDY *keeps topping up* GERALDINE*'s glass.)*

SANDY: That explains why I haven't seen you at the disco before. Was it your first time there?

GERALDINE: Since I got back from Australia, yes.

SANDY: Australia — they're very hard on inverts there.

GERALDINE: Inverts?

SANDY: Well, perhaps perverts is a better word. I like it better. It's more honest, somehow. I hear it ain't easy to be like us down under; no, sir.

146   *Aid Thy Neighbour*

GERALDINE: Well, it's a very interesting country; some of the people there are just like English people, and some are — well, very unconventional, outrageous even.

SANDY: It's the cult of virility, isn't it?

GERALDINE: How do you mean?

SANDY: All that surfin' and struttin' around. *(She strides around the room to make her point.)* It's so *masculine*. Cheers.

GERALDINE *gets up to come over to* SANDY, *who's now by the couch.*

GERALDINE: Cheers, Sandy.

SANDY: Would you mind awfully callin' me John?

GERALDINE: No — no, of course not. It's a nice name.

SANDY: Some of your best friends, eh? Seriously, though, I prefer it at home. It's after Radclyffe.

GERALDINE *(carrying her bag, thinks this might be the beginning of something useful)*: Radclyffe?

SANDY: Radclyffe Hall. 'The Well of Loneliness.'

GERALDINE: Oh — yes. *(But she doesn't really understand.)*

SANDY: Classic dyke novel. I've read it fifteen times. My copy's simply fallin' apart. Don't you just love it?

GERALDINE: Well —

SANDY *(sitting on couch)*: Of course you do. It's our bible.

GERALDINE *(sitting beside her)*: Well, I shall make sure I get my library to order a copy.

SANDY: Oh, Geraldine, you are a card. Radclyffe Hall liked people to call her John. I believe the name ought to be carried on, like a torch. What's your name?

GERALDINE: Archibald?

SANDY: Oh, yes, yes. Tell you what, we'll put that one back in the closet and I'll call you Gerald — just for tonight.

GERALDINE: Gerald will do fine. It's what I'd have liked if I'd been a man. Not, of course, that I would want to have been a man.

She has now casually been able to take the bottle and top up her and SANDY'*s glass, in an effort to get the latter drunk. This is a silent, mutual competition through the rest of the scene.*

SANDY: Oh, this is nice. *(She gets up from the couch and moves* GERALDINE'*s bag away — to the latter's dismay.)* George, dish up the cordon blue. We're famished.

GEORGINA *(from off)*: Coming, coming.

SANDY: Now. I'm sure there are dozens of questions you want to ask us. Feel free.

GERALDINE *(retrieving her bag)*: Well, what I'm really dying to know is why you wanted to have a baby.

SANDY: Straight to the point. Well. The truth is that Georgie decided she wanted to have one. Didn't you, darling?

GEORGINA *(from off)*: What?

SANDY: To be frank, I wasn't bothered one way or the other. But I was prepared to go through it for her, wasn't I, my love?

GEORGINA *(off)*: What's that, Sandy?

GERALDINE: But why did she want to have one?

SANDY: Women want to have babies. It's natural, isn't it? I mean, that's why you're here after all, isn't it. You want to have a baby, just like us?

GERALDINE: Yes, that's right. I do. I've always wanted to have children. All women do, don't they? It's natural.

SANDY: Exactly. Except for me. I don't.

GERALDINE: You've never wanted to have a baby?

SANDY: Never. Perfectly happy as I am. George is very lucky to have me. I shall look after her immaculately.

GEORGINA *enters with a small dish.*

GEORGINA: John is an absolute treasure.

GERALDINE: That looks delicious. Robert Carrier?

GEORGINA: Gertrude Stein. The Alice B. Toklas Cookbook. Kipper paté.

GERALDINE: A woman's right to mousse?

SANDY: Amazin'. I must remember that. *(She and GEORGINA go off into peals of laughter.)* Georgie, I was just telling Gerald here about your desire to breed.

GEORGINA: It's funny, that. I never used to want a baby.

SANDY: I told her, we're all women and some women want to have babies and some don't. *(The doorbell rings, and GEORGINA jumps up to answer it.)*

SANDY: Livin' proof, George is, of the principle that a woman's place is in the home. She has been a transformed woman since I got her in the club.

GERALDINE: That's the other thing I was going to —

SANDY: — ask us about. Eh?

MARY *comes in, dying to be asked to sit down, but GEORGINA comes in after her and takes her tripping off into the kitchen.*

GERALDINE: How did you find a doctor?

SANDY: Oh, contacts. There are a lot of very helpful people about. Look, I'll give you her address now, shall I, before I forget or the evenin' takes over. Got a notebook? *(And she grabs GERALDINE's bag; the latter grabs it back. She takes out a notebook and gives it to SANDY.)*

SANDY: Pen?

GERALDINE *gets a pen from her bag.*

Well, would you believe it. Me mind's gone phut. Blanco.
(GERALDINE goes to take the notebook back.) No, no, leave it, it'll come

back to me. Anyway, it's in me little black notebook in the bedroom. *(Confidentially.)* I can always get it later.

MARY *(popping back)*: Hello. Just popped over to borrow some greaseproof paper. You hadn't got any. Well, 'bye.

She goes.

SANDY: 'Bye, love. Now there's a normal woman. Done a job, settled down, waiting for her family. Just like George. Sometimes I worry about George.

GERALDINE: Why is that?

SANDY: Well — she lacks what I call the necessary feeling of guilt about being a lesbian. Guilt lends it all drama, I feel. You can't be an invert without guilt. There. That's my philosophy in a nutshell.

GEORGINA *(entering)*: Now, have you two been getting to know each other without me?

GERALDINE: Sandy — er, sorry, John — was just beginning to tell me how you arranged to have a baby.

SANDY: Gerald here holds the same views as you, Georgie pet. She has a natural desire to breed.

GEORGINA: John thinks too much. It's all quite simple. Now, let's get down to the important things. Tell us about yourself. I love consciousness-raising over supper. It's so *American*.

GERALDINE: There isn't really a lot to tell.

GEORGINA: Have you always been a journalist?

GERALDINE: For the last five years.

GEORGINA: What about before that?

GERALDINE: Before that — well, I didn't work.

SANDY: Oh, how boredom makin'.

GEORGINA: Why not? I say, have you got a private income?

SANDY: A member of the bourgeoisie in my own home. Whatever next?

GEORGINA: Ignore him, Gerald.

GERALDINE: Well, as I said, there isn't a lot to tell. I've had a really boring life. I'd much rather talk to you about your experiences.

GEORGINA: Oh — how feminist that is.

SANDY: George, would you believe, calls herself a feminist lesbian.

GEORGINA: Lesbian feminist, John.

SANDY: Don't ask me what it means.

GERALDINE: How long have you been together?

GEORGINA: As long as you've been a journalist.

SANDY: Five years, man and girl. Gerald, you must write all this down. Here, let me. *(And she grabs the notebook again.)*

GEORGINA: Come on, what were you doing all those years?

SANDY: Let me guess — I bet — let me see — I bet Gerald was — a housewife.

GEORGINA: No.

SANDY: Am I right or am I right?

GERALDINE: Yes. Actually, I was married.

SANDY: Have a drink, kid.

GEORGINA: And me, John.

SANDY: One glass for you and no more. In your condition. *(GEORGINA simpers.)* I can see it all — married to a pig. *(SANDY now swigs straight from the bottle.)*

GERALDINE: Well, not to start with.

SANDY: Oh no, of course not. Only jokin'.

GERALDINE: He was a journalist. That's how I got into journalism. He helped me.

SANDY: The power behind the throne.

GERALDINE: He was a very successful journalist.

SANDY: They always are, dear.

GERALDINE: Anyway, it didn't work out.

GEORGINA: And then you discovered your true self.

SANDY: That you were a dyke.

GERALDINE: Yes. Yes, that's it.

GEORGINA: And now you live with a woman?

GERALDINE: Er — yes.

SANDY: Gerry — you don't mind me calling you Gerry? Gerry, you are one of the bravest people I've ever met. Tellin' us all about yourself like that. When we were introduced in the disco, I knew we had a lot in common.

GEORGINA: Why didn't it work out?

SANDY: She told you. She discovered her true self. *(As GERALDINE moves up the couch, still clutching her bag, SANDY follows, so that they move up to the other end in tandem.)*

GEORGINA: Did you want a baby then?

GERALDINE: Well — yes, I wanted a baby and he didn't. He didn't want to be tied down.

SANDY: Just like a man, eh?

GEORGINA: He didn't want a family life?

GERALDINE: Yes, that's it. That's it exactly.

SANDY: Not like us, eh? Georgie love? We *are* family life.

GERALDINE: There is another thing —

SANDY: I mean, in the strict bourgeois, legal sense we're not a family, but in practice — well.

GEORGINA: If we were an ordinary married couple —

SANDY: God forbid.

150   *Aid Thy Neighbour*

GERALDINE *(another quip):* When God made man, she was only practising.

Peals of laughter, during which SANDY *shoves* GERALDINE *off the couch onto the floor.*

SANDY: Bet you didn't get that one out of a Christmas cracker, eh?

GEORGINA: As I was saying, if we were an ordinary married couple, John, as the father, would simply put his name on the birth certificate, whether the baby was born by AID or not.

GERALDINE: So actually, the child wouldn't be the legitimate offshoot — I mean, offspring — of the two partners of the marriage?

SANDY *(they are both quite drunk now):* Er, yes, yes. That sounds right. I've never thought of that, have you, Georgie?

GEORGINA: I have read somewhere that up to seventy per cent of the children in Brighton are not fathered by their mothers' husbands.

SANDY: Do you get that, Ger? You don't mind if I call you Ger?

GEORGINA: Or perhaps it was Bournemouth?

GERALDINE: It must be the sea air.

Peals of laughter, during which GERALDINE *crawls round the back of the settee to collect her bag, while* SANDY *follows her round the other side to fill her glass.* GEORGINA *meanwhile grabs a camera and snaps them.*

SANDY: D'you know, her Dad was nearly an Oxford don. What's your Dad?

GERALDINE: A vicar, actually.

SANDY: George, haven't you got a statistic that says 60% of dykes have vicars for fathers? That would explain the guilt.

GERALDINE: So you're saying that lots of children in apparently legitimate, legal marriages — are actually bastards?

GEORGINA: That's right. If you're a married woman and your husband's name is on the birth certificate, in the eyes of the world, the child is legitimate.

GERALDINE: Good Lord. I never thought of that.

SANDY: You see, that's the beautiful thing about us. We don't know who the father is and we don't want to know. George will have her name on the birth certificate and she'll be our baby.

GERALDINE: I wanted a little girl. Little dresses. A doll's house. A fire engine.

GEORGINA: I don't mind if it's a girl or a boy.

SANDY: Think of the advantages we have over your average hetero couple. We know when it's going to be born. We really planned it. None of this messy business about getting pregnant by accident.

GERALDINE *(confidentially to* SANDY*):* When I was married, my mother used to ring up every week and the first thing she'd say was, are you pregnant?

SANDY: Sorry?

GERALDINE: Pardon?

SANDY: Your mother — ?

GERALDINE: I couldn't very well tell her Harry didn't want me to have a baby, could I?

The bell rings.

SANDY: Excuse me. *(But before she can go,* MARY *is in.)*

MARY *(trying to attract* SANDY's *attention to get her out of the room)*: Er — sorry — could I borrow some — er — rubber bands?

SANDY *(too pissed to pick up the hint)*: Help yourself, kid.

MARY: Oh, right. *(She pretends to look round, then tries again to attract their attention, waving.)*

GERALDINE: I mean, you two —

SANDY: 'Bye, Mar'.

MARY *goes off.*

GERALDINE: What I want to know is, how will you bring it up?

GEORGINA *(now snapping away at appropriate points)*: Usual way — nappies, love, milk.

GERALDINE: But doesn't a child need a father.

SANDY: Now I get you. You're worried about what the kid will tell its mates at school, eh?

GERALDINE: If it's a boy, how will it grow up without a model, a male model for behaviour, so's it knows what a man is like?

GEORGINA *snaps.*

What's that?

SANDY: Er — bought her a camera for her birthday. She's just practising. *(To* GEORGINA *— stage whisper.)* Go on, practise. *(To* GERALDINE.) Haven't bought her any film yet.

GERALDINE: How will it know what men are like?

SANDY: Between you and me and this — *(Indicates bottle.)* — most of the models of masculine behaviour you see around are nothing to write home about. It'll have a male model — me.

GERALDINE: I can't imagine a child growing up without a man around.

SANDY: Lots do.

GERALDINE: Where?

SANDY: Things called one-parent families.

GERALDINE: But that's not right, is it?

SANDY: Now take us — me working, Georgie will find a little something to do, make a bit of pin money. *(To* GERALDINE.) You can go on doing your own work, can't you?

GERALDINE: I shan't mind settling down for a while. Save me all those endless battles at work.

SANDY: Battles?

GERALDINE: Men at the top. There's always a man at the top, isn't there?

SANDY: There sure is, kid.

GERALDINE: Harry, my husband — my ex-husband — I would never have got started if it wasn't for him. And do you know, even now, my editor makes me write out a full synopsis of anything I want to write before he commissions me. It's because I'm a woman.

SANDY: Right, right.

GERALDINE: I mean, he'd never say that right out. But I know. Women know.

SANDY: Right. We women really suffer. When I write my autobiography — and I will, be sure I will, I shall call it 'Dyke Unto Death'.

GERALDINE: I've written a novel.

SANDY: What's it about, G., old chap — you don't mind if I call you G.?

GERALDINE: About a woman.

SANDY: Gosh.

GERALDINE: Whose husband doesn't want to have a baby. She gets pregnant by accident. He clears out and leaves her.

SANDY: The cad. I ask you. Would you want your sister to marry one?

GERALDINE: Eh? I haven't got a sister.

GEORGINA: Go on, Gerry.

GERALDINE: Well, she sort of freaks out. I mean, she can't face having a baby on her own.

SANDY: What does she do?

GERALDINE: She has a miscarriage, and when she's lying in the hospital she goes back and relives all the relationships with the men in her life.

GEORGINA: Like a sort of inner voice?

SANDY: G., where did you get those amazing badges?

GERALDINE: Then she kills herself. Throws herself under a train.

SANDY: There should be more train drivers. I mean, more women train drivers.

GERALDINE: A woman's right to choo-choos. *(Both of them think that's hugely funny.)*

SANDY: G., are you one of the feminists we read about in the papers?

GERALDINE: God forbid.

SANDY: G., are you a cynic?

GERALDINE: I'm a realist. What I say is, the way things are is the way things are, right? Go against nature and you let the wild beasts out. John.

SANDY: Yes, G.?

The front door bell rings. GEORGINA *goes.*

GERALDINE: Tell me something.

SANDY: Anything. Are you going to the disco on Friday?

GERALDINE: Who made you a lesbian?

SANDY: The sixty-four thousand dollar query, eh? My mother. And if you buy her the wool, she'll make you one as well.

SANDY *and* GERALDINE *both collapse helplessly on the floor with laughter.*

GERALDINE: John.

SANDY: Mmm?

GERALDINE: I do like your ceiling.

SANDY: It's not at all bad, is it?

GERALDINE: I'd like to lie down on your ceiling.

SANDY: Any special corner?

GERALDINE: If I don't lie down on your ceiling, I shall be sick.

SANDY: Stick with me, kid.

GEORGINA *returns with* MARY *and* JOSEPH, *who survey the debris.*

MARY: I tried to tell you.

GEORGINA: Rubber bands?

MARY: That's right.

JOSEPH: Jesus.

GERALDINE *(flat on the floor)*: Thank you so much for a lovely evening.

SANDY: My pleasure.

JOSEPH: Can you come? We couldn't get hold of anyone else.

GEORGINA: Thanks very much.

JOSEPH: You know what I mean.

MARY: A hundred and one pregnant women all occupying the ante-natal clinic, Georgie.

GEORGINA: I can't leave Sand like this.

MARY: I'll cope, Georgie.

JOSEPH: Come on, we'll get her a taxi.

GEORGINA: Don't forget her bag.

MARY *picks up the bag and gives it to* GEORGINA.

MARY: God, it weighs a ton. What's she got in it?

GEORGINA *opens the bag, takes out the tape recorder.* GEORGINA *takes out the cassette, and replaces the tape recorder in the bag.*

JOSEPH: Come on, Mary.

He and MARY *pick* GERALDINE *up from the floor, supporting her between them.*

GERALDINE *(to* JOSEPH*)*: Hello, Harry.

JOSEPH: Who's Harry?

MARY: Haven't a clue.

GERALDINE *(to* MARY*)*: Hello, Mum.

JOSEPH: Come on. *(They take* GERALDINE *off, followed by* GEORGINA.*)*

GERALDINE *(as she goes)*: It's nice being on the ceiling.

SANDY *(calls after her)*: A woman's right to photograph the news.

Lights dim. Music: 'Show me the way to go home'.

Scene Two

MARY *and* JOSEPH's *bedroom.* MARY *gets into bed and lies down.* JOSEPH *comes in, trying to tread quietly, so as not to wake her.* MARY *groans.*

JOSEPH: Sorry.

MARY: Joe?

JOSEPH: Go back to sleep, love.

MARY: Where are you going? What time is it?

JOSEPH: Five o'clock.

MARY: Have you only just got back?

JOSEPH: They got the police down.

MARY: Oh dear.

JOSEPH: It's alright. They thought it was very funny. Mountains of women sitting around in the middle of the night.

MARY: Joe.

JOSEPH: No disrespect to the mothers-to-be. Most of them have gone home now.

MARY: What happened?

JOSEPH: They have a deputation to the Area Health Authority to discuss the closures.

MARY: What will happen?

JOSEPH: Read the newspapers and find out. God, I'm tired. Goodnight, love.

MARY: You know what today is, don't you?

JOSEPH: I'm going to sleep before today turns into tomorrow.

MARY: D-day. Decision. Do I have my tubes puffed full of gas, do I have the neck of my womb gently stretched, or do I undergo investigative surgery?

JOSEPH: Mary, do you mind, I'm trying to sleep.

MARY: So that I may become pregnant with the aid of a National Health chemistry set.

JOSEPH: Mary, please don't take this the wrong way. I don't mean it the wrong way. I would just like you to remember this conversation next time you tell me women are never irrational.

MARY: If you listened with both ears you would hear the logic echoing through my every syllable. Tomorrow — well, today — is the day we're supposed to decide what further investigation into our infertility we want.

JOSEPH: God, Mary, your grammar.

MARY: Joseph.

JOSEPH: Look, love, I'm exhausted. I've been up all night. We'll talk about it later.

MARY: Was Georgie there all night?

JOSEPH: Till about an hour ago.

MARY: She's pregnant.

JOSEPH: Very observant.

MARY: I hate her.

JOSEPH: You're doing it again.

MARY: I hate her because she's pregnant.

JOSEPH *(resigned)*: Go on.

MARY: She wants a baby.

JOSEPH: That figures.

MARY: And today we have to decide about our baby.

JOSEPH: And how to have our baby.

MARY: What was it like tonight, with all those pregnant women there?

JOSEPH: How do you mean?

MARY: Did you think about what they'd all be doing in a year's time, all of them with their little babies in their little baby-slings?

JOSEPH: Not specially. It was a job. I was taking notes, writing things down.

MARY: I had this funny dream just before you came in.

JOSEPH: Mary, shall I make us some tea?

MARY: Joe, this is serious. There was this person in jeans in the room and then he turned sideways and I saw he was pregnant, like, with this huge stomach. For some reason I just hated him standing here. Then he turned round and had Georgina's face.

JOSEPH: A bad dream.

MARY: And then I thought, whenever Georgina walks into the room and someone asks her when it's due, or puts their hand on her tummy to feel the baby kick, I feel really jealous. I can see me sitting there and you really proud, and me knitting and all of us guessing, is it going to be a boy or a girl. All those corny things that everyone does. And then I try and see myself with a baby, holding it, feeding it, talking to it and the projector breaks down. Nil. Nothing. Nix.

JOSEPH: Why haven't you told me this before?

MARY: I haven't thought of any of it before.

JOSEPH: Came to you, just like that, in a revelation?

MARY: I mean, I really like Georgie.

JOSEPH: So what does it mean?

MARY: I thought wanting to be pregnant and wanting to have a baby were the same thing. They're not.

JOSEPH: Well, they are and they're not.

MARY: For me they're not. I wanted to be pregnant.

JOSEPH: Wanted?

MARY: I don't want a baby, Joe. I don't want to be a mother.

JOSEPH: We've spent a year trying to get pregnant.

MARY: A year trying to get me pregnant.

JOSEPH: Yes. And now you say you don't want to have a baby?

MARY: Yes.

JOSEPH: We could adopt one, if we can't have our own. We've never really talked about that.

MARY: Will you give up your job to look after it?

JOSEPH: Are you asking me to give up my job?

MARY: No. I just want to know how you feel.

JOSEPH: Well, I don't know. I never really thought about it in that way. You were going to be at home.

MARY: Well, I've been at home and I don't like it much.

JOSEPH: But with a baby —

MARY: I don't want a child around all the time.

JOSEPH: What about AID — like Georgie?

MARY: I've had enough of being poked and scraped and peered up. Having a baby's supposed to be natural.

JOSEPH: Having AID's only the doctors helping nature.

MARY: Well, they can help someone else's nature. I don't want a baby.

JOSEPH: I see. *(Pause.)* I do.

MARY: Oh, Joe.

JOSEPH: What am I going to do?

MARY: I don't know. Oh, Joe, I am sorry.

   Music: Alma Cogan singing 'Just Once More'.

Scene Three

GEORGINA *comes on and begins to clear up the debris of the night before.*

GERALDINE *(off)*: Hello.

   GEORGINA *registers.*

GERALDINE *(coming in)*: Hello.

GEORGINA: Geraldine. Hello. Come on in.

GERALDINE: I hope I'm not disturbing you?

GEORGINA: Not at all. Just clearing up. Have a seat. Sorry about the chaos.

GERALDINE: The front door was open, so I just came in.

GEORGINA: We all leave our front doors open. It's very matey here.

GERALDINE: Yes.

GEORGINA: Would you like a drink? Oh, sorry, we did get through rather a lot last night. Coffee?

GERALDINE: No, no thanks.

GEORGINA: Of course. You've come for your jacket.

GERALDINE: I did leave it here?

GEORGINA: In the bedroom. I'll just get it.

GEORGINA *goes out.* GERALDINE *quickly has a search behind the cushions on the couch.*

GEORGINA *(returns)*: There.

GERALDINE: Thanks. *(Pause.)* It was a lovely meal.

GEORGINA: Glad you enjoyed it. Would you like the recipe for the mousse?

GERALDINE: Oh yes. Yes, that would be nice.

GEORGINA: I'll get it. Oh, I nearly forgot. I was going to phone you up, but now you're here, I can show them to you. *(She gets an envelope with some photographs in it.)* Look at that, eh? You and Sandy on the floor. It was a great evening, wasn't it.

GERALDINE: About last night —

GEORGINA: Don't worry about the taxi. We paid him before he left. Look at that. Proper orgy, eh?

GERALDINE: Orgy?

GEORGINA: Oh, Geraldine, you don't remember. Drink does terrible things to the memory, doesn't it?

GERALDINE: What exactly — I mean —

GEORGINA: We had a wonderful time. Quite a landmark for us, last night was.

GERALDINE: Yes, it must have been.

GEORGINA: So when are you going to do it?

GERALDINE: What?

GEORGINA: Follow our shining example. We gave you names, phone numbers, everything.

GERALDINE: Did you?

GEORGINA: Yes, in your little notebook. Oh, Geraldine, you went and left it in the taxi. Honestly.

GERALDINE: It wasn't in my bag.

GEORGINA: Oh dear. Perhaps it dropped out when you got home. You were very merry, Gerry.

GERALDINE: May I have the photos?

GEORGINA: Of course. Just to remind you till next time. You will come round again soon, won't you?

GERALDINE: Of course. Yes, I will.

SANDY *enters, hungover, wearing sunglasses, and with a carrier bag.*

SANDY: Thirteen pounds seventy-two pence for that little lot. Hi, Geraldine. Feeling okay?

GERALDINE: Yes, thanks.

GEORGINA: Geraldine dropped round for her jacket.

SANDY: Oh, right. Want some coffee?

GERALDINE: No thanks, I'm just going.

GEORGINA: I showed Geraldine the photographs and she liked them so much she asked me for them.

SANDY: You gave them to her?

GEORGINA: Well, yes, she was awfully keen.

SANDY: Oh, you're welcome. Georgie can always do some more from the negs. *(GERALDINE reacts.)* Silly you, and you a journalist, eh. Georgie's got the negs. Go on, have a sit. I'll make some coffee. I'm really rather good in the kitchen.

GEORGINA: We have a dark room at the top of the house. Except that I do believe the negs of that little lot aren't here. I believe Sandy took them off somewhere.

SANDY: Oh, my head is killing me. Geraldine, I'm just not used to that sort of thing.

GERALDINE *(still a bit unsure)*: It was a very pleasant evening.

GEORGINA: Geraldine was saying she'd lost her notebook.

SANDY: What, with all the info I relayed? Oh, dear, what a waste.

GERALDINE: I — also wondered — whether I left anything else.

GEORGINA: I don't think so. You left with almost everything you came with.

GERALDINE: Well, I'd better be getting along.

SANDY: Oh, don't go yet. We didn't really finish our conversation last night.

GERALDINE: Which conversation?

SANDY: We talked about everything — life, love, principles, ideals. *(She takes the photos.)* I'd no idea we had so much in common.

GERALDINE: I'm not quite sure I understand you.

SANDY: But perhaps I was wrong. Now, about these negs —

GERALDINE: You were taking photographs all the time.

GEORGINA: Sorry, Geraldine.

SANDY: New camera, she didn't realise there was film in it.

GERALDINE: I don't believe that.

SANDY: Unscrupulous of us, was it?

GERALDINE: To put it mildly.

SANDY: And if, for example, we sold those photographs to some newspaper, with some sort of story, oh, let's say for the sake of argument, a story about how a respectable woman journalist was really a lesbian in her spare time.

GERALDINE: You're joking.

SANDY: Of course I'm joking. It would be quite an unscrupulous thing for us to do and I would hate to have to do it.

GEORGINA: We know how such revelations can ruin a person's career.

SANDY: Not, you understand, because they are perverted and immoral, but because they are thought to be perverted and immoral.

GEORGINA: Sandy and me could explain to you in lots of detail why we think we and lots of other people are neither perverted nor immoral, but I don't think you really want to hear that now, do you?

GERALDINE: I don't understand both of you. Last night —

SANDY: Last night we were a delight. But I'll tell you something. I couldn't lay that sort of act on fulltime.

GEORGINA: Let me try and explain. Say someone, for example, decided to plaster our story all over the middle pages of a newspaper — you know, Lesbian Mums have AID Baby. What would we do?

SANDY: Tell us, George.

GEORGINA: Well, we could go and daub slogans all over the journalist's door, saying 'Lesbian Mums are OK'.

SANDY: We could demand a right of reply in the paper.

GEORGINA: We could demonstrate in the newspaper offices and throw cream buns at the male journalists when they yell 'Burn the Dykes'.

SANDY: We could. Would it ruin our lives, George?

GEORGINA: It would be tough. But no, I don't think it would ruin our lives. We have had a lot of vicissitudes.

SANDY: What a super word. You've been reading again, haven't you?

GERALDINE: How did you find out between last night and today?

SANDY: Give us credit, Geraldine.

GERALDINE: I bet I know who it was.

GEORGINA: It doesn't matter who it was. What I'd like to know is — was it all true — about your marriage?

GERALDINE: Yes. Yes, it was.

GEORGINA: So you were quite — frank — with us?

GERALDINE: Yes. As far as that went.

SANDY: But you don't want to have a baby.

GERALDINE: Yes, I do. I'm a normal woman. I want to marry and —

SANDY: That's alright, Geraldine, we're not prejudiced against heterosexuals.

GEORGINA: We wouldn't dream of trying to stop you. Sandy, perhaps we're jumping to conclusions. Perhaps we're mis-judging Geraldine. Geraldine, I appeal to you as a woman —

GERALDINE: You certainly don't appeal to me as a woman.

SANDY: Ah. Well, that's not quite how it seemed last night.

GEORGINA: You don't feel any sympathy for us?

GERALDINE: I can't feel any kind of sympathy for what you're doing. It goes against all I believe in.

SANDY: Against your moral code?

GERALDINE: It's not my code. It's everyone's moral code.

SANDY: I wouldn't say that. Indeed, I would say that it was full of holes, your moral code.

GEORGINA: Hang on, Sand. Geraldine, you can understand me wanting to have a baby, can't you?

GERALDINE: Yes. I think so.

GEORGINA: And Mary, next door, she may well have a baby by AID. So what's the difference?

GERALDINE: You know very well what's the difference.

SANDY: So you still plan to write the articles?

GERALDINE: I shall decide that myself.

GEORGINA: Well, that's a real pity, isn't it, Sand. Because we'll have to start getting some names and addresses ourselves and sending some six by eights through the post and we all know how much a first-class stamp costs these days. Black or white coffee?

GERALDINE: You are both quite shameless.

GEORGINA: Now look here. Last night was, as Sandy says, very hard work. And when I get round to thinking about it properly, I shall probably feel very ashamed of the fact that it was necessary in the first place. It's entirely up to you.

GERALDINE: If I don't write it, someone else will. There's someone else working on it as well.

GEORGINA: No, there isn't.

GERALDINE: You should think about the child. About its life. You can't keep it secret forever. People will know, the public has a right to know.

SANDY: Fine. You tell them about us and we'll tell them about you. With photographs. Was her jacket in the bedroom, Georgie?

GERALDINE: You really are disgusting. What you did last night was beyond belief.

SANDY: Was it? What did we do?

GEORGINA: I don't think she can remember it all.

GERALDINE: You're messing around with other people's lives — you're going to bring a child into the world —

SANDY: We know.

GERALDINE: To satisfy your own selfish whims.

GEORGINA: It isn't a game, Geraldine.

GERALDINE: Well, you've got the world against you.

SANDY: Except for you. You can't afford to be against us. Not in print, anyway. A woman's right to lose, eh, Geraldine?

GERALDINE: Well, you can keep your perverted little lives. And I'll tell you one more thing: if I had the choice, I would rather give a child to a pair of homosexual men than to a pair of hysterical dykes.

GERALDINE grabs the photos and storms out.

GEORGINA: I don't think we'll ask her to babysit, eh?

Scene Four

SANDY, MARY and JOSEPH come on. DAPHNE comes on carrying curtains.

MARY: Oh, Sandy, I wish I'd been there.

SANDY: You tried your best to be.

MARY: I was making damson preserve.

DAPHNE: It sounds like a night to remember.

GEORGINA enters; JOSEPH jumps up to give her his seat.

JOSEPH: May I have a feel?

GEORGINA: Be my guest.

JOSEPH *(hand on her tum)*: He's very quiet tonight.

DAPHNE: He?

JOSEPH: I have second sight. Feminine intuition.

GEORGINA: Nonsense, it's a girl.

SANDY: I bet it's twins.

MARY: Sandy was just telling us about last night — and I *did* need some rubber bands. Well. Now it's my turn to make a speech.

Ooohs and Aaahs of congratulations.

Well, thank you all very much, but I'm not. Again.

Ooohs and Aaahs of commiseration.

DAPHNE: I have some news as well — a denouement to delight your hearts.

SANDY: Geraldine Kramer — alias Marshall — is going to send us a letter of apology.

DAPHNE: Ever the optimist, Sandy. I have heard, on the grapevine, you understand, that she's going abroad.

GEORGINA: But what's she going to do?

DAPHNE: She's left the paper and gone off on holiday, and I'm pretty sure she's given up the idea of doing the story. She's going back to — where was it —

SANDY: Australia.

DAPHNE: There you are then.

JOSEPH: What did you do with the notebook?

SANDY: Put it with the cassette and I do believe George accidentally dropped them both in the dustbin.

MARY: Oh, I think you did wonderfully.

SANDY: She'll live to write another day.

GEORGINA: Pity. I quite liked her.

SANDY: George.

GEORGINA: I'm sure there was really a nice woman there underneath.

JOSEPH: She'll be using lots more cassettes in her career.

GEORGINA: I know.

MARY: You still haven't heard my news properly.

SANDY: We're really sorry, Mary.

MARY: So am I.

SANDY: What for?

MARY: I've been quietly hating Georgina for months. Five months and two weeks, to be precise. Not you as a person, just you as a pregnant being. I don't hate you any more.

GEORGINA: What have I done?

MARY: Nothing. That's what I'm trying to say. It's me.

GEORGINA: But I'm still pregnant.

MARY: Yes. And I've gone back on the pill.

SANDY: Joseph, what have you done to her?

JOSEPH: Don't blame me, this is all her own work.

GEORGINA: But what about —

SANDY: What about Joe?

JOSEPH: She's left me holding the baby. Or rather not holding the baby. High and dry without even a motorbike to call my own.

MARY: When I go back to work, I'll put a down payment on one for you.

SANDY: Now I've heard everything.

MARY: Not quite everything. You know how people sometimes say 'I woke up to the fact'? Well, that's just what I did, didn't I, Joe? I suddenly thought, I don't want to be a mother. And then I realised that wanting to be a mother is a bit like wanting to be a nun. If you haven't got a vocation, you lie awake at night wishing you had one; and then when you've got one, you lie awake at night wondering whether you're living up to it.

JOSEPH: My wife the intellectual.

SANDY *(to* JOSEPH*)*: I really will teach you to ride my bike.

JOSEPH: I don't think somehow it's the same thing.

DAPHNE: Oh, come on, Joe, stiff upper lip. Maybe Mary will change her mind.

MARY: I've decided for now.

JOSEPH: Oh, here. I nearly forgot. *(He takes the list off the wall and gives it to* GEORGINA.*)*

GEORGINA: What's that?

JOSEPH: All my friends who said they'd babysit. You may as well have it. It took a lot of getting. *(He adds a name.)* There. Me as well.

GEORGINA: Oh, Joe, I can't bear it.

DAPHNE: They won't do it, you know. Most people don't like other people's children.

JOSEPH: Well, maybe I'll be the lone shining exception. I warn you, Mary, you haven't heard the last of this.

MARY: We'll see.

DAPHNE: Well, now it's my turn. *(She stands up and displays the curtains. They all make admiring noises.)*

GEORGINA: Since when have you taken up needlecraft?

DAPHNE: They're from my Auntie Ivy. I told her you needed curtains in your kitchen. I measured the windows last week.

SANDY: Great. Thanks.

DAPHNE: I'll put them up. Then I thought I could measure the bathroom. Now listen. I've had this deliciously amazing idea. Are you ready?

SANDY: Last time you had an amazing idea I ended up with the biggest hangover in the world.

DAPHNE: Well, this one's just as good. Now. You two have got far more rooms than you need. Lucy and I could have the two rooms at the top, next to George's darkroom, and you'd still have a room for the baby and a spare. And then I thought, Lucy could go to school with Sandy in the mornings and Georgina would be here in the afternoons when Lucy gets back from school. What do you think?

GEORGINA: She wants to move in.

SANDY: Does she really?

GEORGINA: She seems to.

DAPHNE: Lucy loves babies and she could babysit.

GEORGINA: Now that is an interesting proposition.

DAPHNE: And then I thought — this wall — we could knock it down and have one huge living room between the two houses and Joe needn't run all the way round when he comes to babysit.

SANDY: She had me interested before — but this is something else.

MARY: Daphne, do you mean one of those commune places?

DAPHNE: That was just an example —

GEORGINA: Sandy, have you ever thought about being a landlady?

SANDY: I can't say as I have. But I'm a very open-minded sort of person.

DAPHNE: Well, it's only an idea, and we don't want to rush into anything. But term will be over soon and next year Lucy will be in Middlesi know how long it takes to get keys cut —

SANDY *and* GEORGINA *quieten her with a huge hug — * JOSEPH *comes over to join them, and* MARY *gets up, holding a midnight blue baby's sweater. She drops it.*

MARY: Oh dear. It's funny, I never used to drop things when I was at work. Odd, isn't it? Georgina, do you like midnight blue?

She hands the sweater over to GEORGINA *who turns it round and holds it against her stomach. On the back is knitted the feminist symbol of a fist in a circle. Alma Cogan sings* 'You, Me and Us'.